MW01067671

LIVE YOUR DREAMS OUT LOUD

6 STEPS TO CONQUER YOUR FEARS
AND ACHIEVE YOUR DREAMS

Brian D. Johnson

Live Your Dreams Out Loud Publishing Los Angeles

Harriet Tubman said,

"Every great dream begins with a dreamer. Always remember, you have within you the strength, the patience, and the passion to reach for the stars to change the world."

I dedicate this book to my mother and brother. I love you two with all of my heart and appreciate your support while on this journey to live my dreams and change the world.

Contents

CHAPTER 1
Clarity / 31
Clarity and Quieting the Noise to Find Your Dream

CHAPTER 2
Commitment / 51
Commitment and Owning Your Dream

CHAPTER 3
Connections / 67
Master the Art of Connections

CHAPTER 4
Competence / 95
Competence and Becoming World-Class

CHAPTER 5
Conditioning / 113
Conditioning Yourself to Chase Your Dream

CHAPTER 6
Cash Flow / 131
Cash Flow and Resourcing Your Dream

Acknowledgments

Throughout the course of this dream journey, I've met and become friends with so many wonderful people. I've been blessed to work alongside some of the biggest names in entertainment and seek advice on the how. I've been fortunate to interview and become friends with the who's who around the globe. I would be remiss if I didn't acknowledge that I didn't go at this journey alone. Every conversation, every person, every volunteer, intern, my family and friends; I sincerely want to say thank you. This book was made possible because of you. If we've ever met, became friends or worked together, your energy is a contribution to this book being completed.

Before We Get Started; Lets Meet!

 As the Founder of Live Your Dreams Out Loud Movement; I have spent the last 5 years living my dream to inspire as many entrepreneurs as possible. As such; I have curated content in order to provide aspiring entrepreneurs the resources they need to live their dream. I wanted to provide you the opportunity to experience some of these resources for yourself as a companion to this book. I hope you enjoy watching and listening as much as I have enjoyed creating them.

My weekly show; The Dreamer Series will introduce you to dreamers just like yourself all over the country. The Live Your Dreams Out Loud Podcast is a really deep dive with entrepreneurs from all across the world. You can find both of these shows here: **Liveyourdreamsoutloud.com/shows**

If you are a dreamer that meet the criteria and want to be featured on one of my shows that I host, please visit **Liveyourdreamsoutloud.com** and click on shows to pitch yourself.

As a personal development coach, I also provide free webinars and training sessions all year long for entrepreneurs. Please visit **Liveyourdreamsoutloud.com/free-training** to get immediate access to the trainings. Finally, if you want to join and connect with a diverse set of dreamers from around the globe, join the free Live Your Dreams Out Loud Community at **Facebook.com/LiveYourDreamsOutLoud**

For all other questions and concerns, please email me at **info@liveyourdreamsoutloud.com**

Preface

This book is for everyday dreamers.

A dreamer is anybody who challenges the norm.

A dreamer puts their ideas and thoughts to the test.

Dreamer's aren't afraid to take risks.

Dreamer's see the world through a different lens.

A dreamer is intuitive and visualizes and is constantly thinking of a way to be BETTER.

A dreamer thrives on inspiration and has the motivation to create.

If you aspire to call yourself an entrepreneur, a conscious creator, dreamer, thought leader, author, speaker, athlete, change agent, a future interior designer, world traveler, bakery owner, personal trainer, or future lawyer—whoever you dream to be—this book is for you.

Let me be clear: if right now you are not where you want to be, but you don't know where to start, then we are going to change your life. We are going to identify your path and conquer any fear you might have about living your dream. If you don't know how to go about the process and what the process entails, or if you are struggling with the how to live your dreams out loud this book is for you. I am going to give you the inspiration, the motivation, and the specific steps you need. From this day forward, we will face your fears and begin to live your dreams out loud.

No matter your age, financial status, bad hand that you've been dealt or socioeconomic status, if you have a dream, this book is for you. Dreams come in many different sizes and shapes. We are living in a century with a world's worth of information right before our eyes and at our fingertips. With that in mind, you need to know that it's never too late to start living out your dream.

When I started out conceptualizing this book, I concentrated my thoughts on the reader. The first edition of this book inspired thousands to live out their dreams, and I'm hoping the insights I've gained over the past five years will continue to serve others in this second edition.

My lifelong dream has always been to inspire, educate and entertain people to live their best life by giving them the proper resources to do so. Early on, I believed that as a TV host, global speaker, author, and thought leader, I could affect millions of people in a positive way. I knew that by pursuing my dream, I could in turn help others achieve theirs. Diversity and inclusion is deeply rooted into my mission. It's important that through my works, I give people the human experience to expose and break the preconceived notions and stereotypes that one may have of others. A difference of opinions, logic and implementation will spur change for dreamers around the world for generations to come.

Since writing the first edition in 2014, my dream of launching a TV show (*The Dreamer Series*), writing a book, speaking around the country, and building a business as a thought leader has come to fruition. How did I make all that happen? As cliché as it may sound, I made a decision and a commitment to take action, and I will show you how to do the same. Authoring this book was part of the foundation for all of those things coming to fruition, and it has changed my life forever. I knew I needed to share my mess—and eventually my message—to other dreamers out there who want to live their dreams out loud. The emails, messages, and standing ovations I've received have validated why my story, and this book, matters. Here are some important things I've learned along the way:

- You don't have to be the best at something in order to help others.
- You don't have to have money to help others.
- You don't need money to begin.
- Most people have a desire to achieve a long-held dream, like writing a book, but they never do, because of fear, laziness, or both)
- There are so many people with stories, a certain expertise, skill, or knowledge who NEVER act upon those things.

When people consider what it would take to live out their dreams, they immediately conjure some romantic notion of quitting jobs, following passions, and everything turning out just fine. It would appear that anything less would mean you aren't serious about living your dream. Truth is, there is more than one way to go about living your dreams. You have to do what's best for you. Even though I knew I had a responsibility to share my truth in this book, that didn't make it easy. My struggle with continuously working full-time in television production versus going "all in" and not working for anybody else has been challenging. However, it didn't make me any less committed to my dreams, and the same goes for you. Remember, your "all in" can be different from somebody else's.

The research process for this book was based on several elements: my own journey as a personal development coach and mentor to hundreds of everyday dreamers, reading books, attending conferences, interviewing thought leaders, and working in an industry alongside some of the most successful entertainers of our time. I also surveyed thousands of everyday dreamers and asked them this, "What's the number one thing that's holding you back from living your dreams?" Their answers, combined with everything I learned and researched, are contained in this book, which is what I hope will be a comprehensive guide for you to live your dreams.

2014- 2019

Before we move forward, we need to take a quick flashback. I have learned so much in the last five years, and I want to take you on a quick ride so that many of the stories and the individuals I discuss in this book make sense. I'll go as quickly as I can, so hang on!

I was working on the *Arsenio Hall Show* several years ago, and the show ended while I was finishing the first edition of this book. At that time, I was also preparing for a nationwide media and book tour and getting ready to launch Season 1 of the Live Your Dreams Out Loud podcast. In just a short eighteen months since I had arrived in Los Angeles, I was working alongside some of the biggest names in entertainment while being mentored from some of the most influential individuals in the world. It was time to begin the process of living my dreams as a thought leader. My foundational message was all about the process of living your dreams. I wanted to take my best practices and tips and give them to other dreamers.

I launched the book, and I was off to the races, speaking, developing educational content online, and building my brand as the Chief Dreamer. Shortly after launching the LYDOL brand, I got a call from a former associate about an opportunity of a lifetime. They asked if I had any interest in working on a new show starring Bill Nye on Netflix. The position involved overseeing the talent and working with Bill on a daily basis, and there was no way I could pass that up.

When I started the Bill Nye Show, I was working full-time on the Live Your Dreams Out Loud brand. I had been booking and producing the podcast myself. Taking the job with the Bill Nye Show meant that I needed to give the podcast a break. I could have continued producing the podcast, but I felt I needed to focus on the gig and learn what I needed to learn on this show. What ended up happening as a result of my work on the Bill Nye Show was a chance meeting with Janell Barrett Jones— someone who would share my vision and provide the support I needed. I told her about all my dreams and plans within a few days of meeting her.

Janell and I build a friendship that eventually became a business partnership. We set out across the country and filmed 62 episodes of The Dreamer Series in 11 cities. How did that all happen? Through connecting, which we'll talk more about later. A relationship from Arsenio Hall led me to Bill Nye, and a relationship with Bill Nye led me to my business partner and realizing my dream of hosting my show. As I write this today, The Dreamer Series episodes are released weekly on Instagram, YouTube and Facebook as well our recently secured distribution onto iTunes, Roku, and Google Play via our distributor The Knekt Network. All these experiences led to my work on the Emmy-winning Carpool Karaoke for Apple/CBS.

How does this relate to you? How does a dreamer start to live out loud? A dreamer is anybody who challenges the norm and is ok with going against it. A dreamer puts one's ideas and thoughts to the test. Dreamers aren't afraid to take risks. Dreamers see the world through a different lens. A dreamer is intuitive and is constantly thinking of a way to be better. A dreamer thrives on inspiration and creation. One misconception is that dreamers are lazy and fail to take action. That's why it's important to not just be a dreamer and "live the dream" but to also take action and live out loud. Living Your Dreams Out Loud is all about identifying your dreams, recognizing opportunities, and taking action.

As kids, we hear that we should dream big and that we can do anything we put our minds to. We lose that notion somewhere along the path to adulthood. I chose this particular subject of being a dreamer because the meaning of life is to live fully and wholly. Some of us believe we don't have the skills and knowledge to act on our dreams. I am here to teach you that is not true.

My clients often say they feel a certain stigma that surrounds the concept of "chasing a dream." That stigma mistakenly embraces the concept that a dreamer is someone who merely wishes for something to happen—that dreamers aren't action-takers. Friends and family may tell a dreamer that his or her head is stuck in the clouds and that the dreamer is too slow to take action — that their dream isn't "realistic."

Some of the greatest ideas and dreams are in the graveyard because some dreamers never acted upon their desires and never allowed themselves to fully live. There is tremendous beauty in life once you discover its true meaning and walk your path. You are doing the world and others a disservice if you don't act on your passions and dreams. I strongly believe those innate desires are purposeful and intended for you to act upon them. We are servants. Life's purpose is to serve, to add value, and to act on the desires of your heart.

I have tangible success with living my dreams out loud, and I want you to gain perspective from my journey. I want you to take action and live your dreams out loud the way you want to. I'm not saying my process is the only answer—I'm suggesting it can serve as a blueprint for anybody with a dream. You can look at my process and learn from what has worked (and what hasn't). I'm sharing all of my setbacks, disappointments, jubilant highs and crushing blows.

You will learn my journey involved a combination of getting clear about my dreams and finding ways to constantly have the discipline to act on them. I've learned I can inspire and motivate others to act on their dreams. Regardless of what I do, you still have to do it yourself. One of the keys to success lies in finding somebody who's already been successful at what you are doing, study them, and act on what you've learned. You will learn more about this in the coming chapters.

My goal with this book is to provide you with the necessary

steps to move from thoughts to actionable habits and to live your dreams out loud! This stems from a personal calling to take action and to create something valuable that outlives me and motivates others to live their dreams for generations to come. I discovered my purpose and mission years ago: to help and serve others through motivation and inspiration while being the best human I can be here on earth.

There are millions of other books out there that are life-changing. As an author and avid reader, it has been a challenge for me not to compare my writings to others. In that spirit, I similarly challenge you not to compare your dreams and process to anybody else's. You were created on purpose for a purpose.

It is no exaggeration to say that I genuinely want to change your life.

LIVING YOUR DREAMS OUT LOUD

is all about

IDENTIFYING YOUR DREAMS, RECOGNIZING OPPORTUNITIES, *and* TAKING ACTION.

About this book

I commend you for buying a book like this because it speaks to your commitment. Not everyone is brave enough to admit that their current experience of life is not enough for them. More importantly, making a statement like that makes it impossible to keep living the same way. It forces you to change. You're not crazy—you're simply different than most people. Those feelings you're feeling aren't just discontent; they represent the real you. These feelings scream from your belly, encouraging you to live the life you were meant to live. No amount of money and no amount of comfort will ever make those feelings go away. Trust me, I've tried. There's only one antidote: living your dreams out loud.

You didn't pick up this book by accident. Chances are, there is some reason this topic matters to you. Maybe you're looking for inspiration. Maybe you are a dreamer and want to know how you can begin to live out your dreams. You might be disillusioned with your job or up to your eyeballs in debt. Maybe your significant other left you—again. Whatever your story, you need to be honest with yourself about why you may be at this crossroads.

After interviewing and surveying hundreds of people, I was able to discern the six major reasons people feel too afraid to pursue their dreams. These are the questions and concerns that tend to hold us back:

1. **Starting.** *I have so many ideas and visions but where do I start?*
2. **Uncertainty.** *How will I know I am pursuing the right dream once I get started?*
3. **Stability.** *Will I still be able to support my family when pursuing this dream?*
4. **Age.** *Am I too old to pursue this dream?*
5. **Work-life balance.** *How do I balance a job that pays the bills while working on my dreams?*
6. **Perception.** *What will people think when I pursue my dream vs. what they are used to seeing me do?*

I understand those fears, and I used to share those same worries until I learned how to confront and overcome those fears by taking specific actions, which I'm going to share with you. Throughout this book, I will outline and detail the **6 Steps to Living Your Dreams Out Loud**. Mastery of these steps leads to the development of these steps as habits, and when you've adopted these good habits, you'll be well on your way to living your dreams out loud.

The pages you hold in your hands will help you to do the following:

The pages you hold in your hands will help you to:

- Understand how my journey led to my discovery.
- Develop strategies to help you achieve your dreams.
- Reflect on your own journey.

- Actively begin to create your strategic plan.
- Gain the confidence you need to aggressively implement these lessons.

Throughout the book, I invite you to share what you're learning with me and the **Live Your Dreams Out Loud** community on the blog at **www.LiveYourDreamsOut loud.com #LYDOL**. I read every comment, and I cannot wait to see how you use this book to make your dreams come true.

Thank you for taking this journey.

All my best,
Brian Johnson

The Beginning of Brian Johnson

We all have a beginning. My beginning starts in a single-wide trailer with a hard-working mother, a younger brother and an absent father. The first chapter of my life growing up with little means, in an area steeped in racial history, will forever affect the way I view the world.

Unfortunately, my parents split when I was around three years old. My mother worked multiple jobs to ensure that my brother and I were always taken care of. She never complained and never put herself before us. My mother's commitment to my brother and I has always been amazing, and I am forever grateful for that. My mother often went without so that my brother and I could thrive. I am deeply motivated by the desire to provide my mom with a better life. In fact, it has always been my primary goal to take care of my mother and to make her the proudest mother on earth. Her level of commitment has stuck with me and will for the rest of my life. It is the kind of dedication necessary for following and achieving your dreams.

I grew up in Skipperville, Alabama, where the rooster from my neighbor Joe McNair's yard would begin to sound off religiously at six in the morning. Skipperville is a small town in the southeast corner of Alabama where the population (at the time) was between 500 and 600 people. Skipperville is made up of hard-working, mostly blue-collar individuals who take pride in traditional values, family and community. The make-up of the town includes a K-12 school, a post office and a convenience store. It is truly what you think of when you envision "the country." In order to get to the closest grocery store or fast-food restaurant, you have to drive 15 to 20 minutes into the city.

A lot of people who grew up in my town were small-minded in their beliefs. The environment in which they were raised coupled with cultural conditioning and the history of Alabama are factors that kept them from being more open-minded.

Many people's traditional mindset is due to the history of the South, which in turn is the driving force for their logic and actions. The Civil Rights Act had been passed twenty years prior to my birth, but that is a short span of time for an ideology that had been passed down through generations.

This racially-divided belief system is deeply rooted in our country's history, particularly in Alabama as one of the confederate states. Conservative history led to—and still leads to—conservative thoughts.

My inner voice always told me not everyone in the world thought the same way people around me did. I was determined to break free from that specific environment of hatred that I witnessed because of the color of my skin.

As early as I can remember, I felt different because I was black. My family has never exuded prejudice; it's always been about protection from those who wanted to harm us because we were black. I was even taught how to act if I ever got pulled over by the police.

In all honesty, it is a challenge for me to share some of the ugly truths about the place where I grew up. As many negative situations as I may have encountered, I also have fond memories, and many of the people I grew up with are friends to this day.

My struggle is that I feel as if I would be doing you a disservice if I didn't share my truth about my upbringing. I'm not saying that everyone in my town was racist, but the climate there sure did weather a certain storm that remains consistent.

These challenges, however, were mostly geared around the mindset of certain individuals who spewed their dislike of me due to the color of my skin. I've educated myself on how to deal with racism and the many ways it can manifest itself. Since it's intuitively in my wheelhouse to bring humans together from all different walks of life to experience each other, I have found this to be my way of contributing to a solution.

My first dream

It's hard to become what you don't see, and in Skipperville, I didn't see much. My surroundings didn't look like anything that I had dreamed and imagined. Growing up in a small town, I saw first-hand what happens to people when they don't have access to resources and inspiration. But the common way of living life (finishing school, getting a job in the local area, having a family, worrying about money all the time, and dying) didn't look like the way I wanted to live life. It didn't feel like it was what I was supposed to do. Dealing with racism and other things, I instinctively knew there had to be a better way.

Television and the internet ignited the spark of possibilities for me. I saw professional athletes who looked like me on TV, and they were playing a sport that I loved. Michael Jordan was my hero. The TV and the internet gave me access to watching live games, and I began to see the world in different ways beyond my imagination. I loved television, and intuitively I knew that basketball and TV were somehow going to play significant roles in my life. Having access to shows like The Oprah Winfrey Show, SportsCenter with Stuart Scott, and The Arsenio Hall Show let me see and truly know that I could make my dreams my reality.

I spent a few Alabama summers with my Aunt Doretha and her five sons (my cousins) in Daleville, Alabama (25 miles from Skipperville). They lived in the housing authority, which was located next door to the high school and community center.

I wasn't the only dreamer in the family. I had a cousin, Shaun, in Daleville who was also filled with inspiration and talent. Daleville was a much bigger city than Skipperville; they actually had grocery stores and a McDonalds. It was there in Daleville that I got a chance to see Shaun's true gift and talent as a human and basketball player. He was so much better than anyone else. He was 6'5" but played and jumped as if he was 7 feet tall. He had the sweetest jump-shot ever and was a great ball player. High school athletes who don't pass their college boards can attend a community or junior college, boost their academic achievements there, and then transfer to a four-year college or university, and that's what Shaun did. He attended

Chattahoochee Valley Community College, and after excelling and breaking records at the junior college, he was on the verge of signing with a four-year college in Georgia. He was about to make his dream a reality.

At the time, Shaun was dating a girl in Enterprise, Alabama. Shaun and two of his brothers, Marcus and Maurice, were visiting his girlfriend. Shaun took his then-girlfriend to get some diapers, and when he came back to drop her off at the house, he walked her to the door. Her baby's father pulled up in the driveway and pretended as if everything was ok, but the situation quickly escalated from something slightly awkward at best to violent at worst. He shot my cousin Shaun several times, and he died at the scene. Marcus tried to grab the gun away from him but was shot in the stomach. It was a tough loss for my family, the community, and for those who loved Shaun.

Personally, I was already feeling the pain of not having my father around, and the impact of losing Shaun compounded the weight on my heart, making the pain unbearable.

Basketball became my chosen therapy, and as the years went by, I went to college, played collegiate basketball, graduated, and got a "good" job.

My first job after college, I worked with a Fortune 500 company as a territory sales manager overseeing a territory that was doing $27 million dollars in revenue. I took the job because all my friends were accepting high-paying jobs from Fortune 500 companies, going to law school, and following the traditional path to success. It seemed fitting that I, too, pursued the highest-paying and most sought-after job. At the time, I still didn't know what I wanted to do when I accepted the job, but I knew I wanted to explore as many opportunities as possible until I could figure it out.

After accepting that job, I ended up sick and miserable. I made frequent trips to the doctor whose only diagnosis was that I was under high loads of stress. I received prescriptions for Zyprexa, but I never took any. I hated my job so much that I would wake up in tears.

After consistent days of waking up in misery, applying for other jobs without any luck, and undergoing minor procedures with a camera down my stomach to be told "it's nothing but stress," I was terminated for something that I didn't have any control over. I know that this is a common occurrence—this has probably happened to many of you out there! It still came as a blow, however, since I didn't have any clarity about what I wanted to do with my life, and I didn't know where to start besides with constant prayer. I realized I hadn't had control of my professional destiny, and that scared me to death. (I know being fired from a job can feel like the end, but often than not it can be the kick in the pants and the start you need to begin living your dreams. Keep that in mind, dreamers.)

Have you ever chased the money and ignored your gut? I've done it, and I know plenty of people who have done the very same. I allowed my external influences dictate my truth, and the truth was that I should have listened to myself. There was no need for me to be like everybody else. I succumbed to my surroundings instead of listening to my internal voice, which remained constant. I knew in my soul that I was not on the right path, but I ignored it until I couldn't ignore it anymore. I very quickly started to spiral into depression and was repeatedly hospitalized, until one day, I finally tried to take my own life.

In that moment, I had to make a decision: either end it all or get on my path to inspire others and never look back.

September 2011, I-285, Atlanta, Georgia

The moment I almost ended my dream forever

If we bury who we truly are and who we truly desire to be long enough, that piece of us begins to diminish. It seems like it grows quiet, but it simply simmers below the surface until it becomes a dull roar. That's what my life had eventually become.

I understand what it's like to harbor a long-held dream and then feel it draining away from you. I know how the pains of life can feel more like dead-end signs than detours. And I remember the day I faced a life-changing decision: I was either going to end it all or start living my dream out loud.

It was the fall of 2011. My consultancy job had dried up, my girlfriend and I had gone through an unbelievably bad break-up, and the car that I nearly crashed was on the verge of being repossessed. It was like I was literally losing everything. I was living so quietly that my life was on the verge of becoming completely silent.

I remember that day vividly:

I'm driving, but it feels like I'm floating above myself and watching a movie. There are blurry objects everywhere. Without a real destination in mind, I swerve around them wildly. I come within feet of smacking dead into a blue car. It doesn't register that there are other cars on the road and that I'm on the freeway. I see white—my knuckles. How long have I been gripping this steering wheel? Damn, that music is loud! Still, my thoughts are louder: I'm not letting up. Not this time.

Decision made: this time I'm taking it all the way. At the very next exit I see, I am going to crash this car right into a wall and end it all.

Immediately, I can see my mom. This would destroy her. I can see my brother delivering the news and her sobbing uncontrollably. She falls to her knees wondering what she did wrong or what more she could've done.

There's no time for empathy now. This is it.

I press on the gas just a little more. That's it, 120 mph. I take off my seat belt (can't take any chances). Why is that damn music still on?

> **I just need time alone with my own thoughts, /**
> **Got treasures in my mind but couldn't**
> **open up my own vault, /**
> **My childlike creativity, purity, and honesty/**
> **Is honestly being crowded by these grown thoughts, /**
> **Reality is catching up with me, taking my inner child/**
> **I'm fighting for custody, /**
> **With these responsibilities that they entrust in me. /**

I swear I'd heard those lyrics a thousand times, but for one reason or another, this time, they seemed to reach out from the radio through my chest and take full grip of my heart. Kanye West's *"Power"* had been screaming at me, trying to break through my desperate thoughts.

Something in those lyrics triggered something: there is promise in me. I have ideas, goals, and dreams to actualize. The monotony of daily life had drowned them out. *Wake up, work on my dreams, look for new clients, no luck, girlfriend drama, bills, go to sleep, repeat.* My passions and my inner child-like creativity were screaming for help. I was indeed fighting for custody of my own identity, and in that moment in time, I most certainly was not winning.

Apparently, I'd been driving toward my apartment complex. I exited the freeway, parked my car, and swung the door open. Hysterical and fighting back tears, I ripped off my sweat-stained shirt and threw it in the dumpster. Half-naked and overwhelmed, I fell to my knees, lifted my hands, and begged for forgiveness and direction.

In that moment, I made the most pivotal decision of my life: from now until my last breath, I would live a life full of service and fulfill my purpose by using all my God-given talents to inspire generations to come by LIVING MY DREAMS OUT LOUD.

Life has a way of challenging us, and overcoming those challenges ultimately strengthens and improves our lives. We are all vessels, and we can use these challenges not only to help ourselves but also to help others. Opening up and sharing my story has helped heal me, and I know that it's helped others, too. Now, most of us don't like to share our emotions or our struggles—we view them through a lens of weakness instead of opportunities to grow.

Here's the real talk: if you are battling any kind of depression, seek out professional help. If you're struggling but you're not sure why, it could be that you have undiagnosed mental health issues and don't have the right tools in place to overcome the trauma of life's shifts and turns. (I personally still have anxiety issues, and I deal with the panic attacks when they come. I take preventative measures so they don't arise, but I'm glad that I understand my mental health challenges and that I have tools in place if an episode occurs.) Therapy has been beneficial for me in a lot of ways, and it can be for you too. You don't have to fight these emotions and situations by yourself. Get some help!

On that September day, I saw that I was on a path of discovery, trying to live out my purpose for being on this earth. Nothing was working, and I had lost material things that really didn't matter. I lost love, too, which did matter. When my girlfriend and I broke up, it broke the proverbial camel's back (Hint: I was the camel.) I had invested so much into her and into the relationship to the point of even jeopardizing myself and not being responsible. For that break-up to happen during a time when it seemed like everything else was going wrong was the last thing I expected. It brought me to a place I'd never experienced. Looking back now, everything that I went through was all for a reason; it was preparation for my future, and God had to clear my path so I could fly.

Have you ever felt as if everything in life is not going right for you? If you are having a tough time with life and it seems as if everything is going the wrong way, pull the book a little closer and listen to what I'm about to tell you. No matter how empty or rock-bottom things seem to be, taking your life isn't the solution.

If you are alive, then there is hope. If you are alive, then you have a choice. The first word in this book is to LIVE. If you have life, then you can seriously change your situation in spite of what it may seem like, and you can choose to LIVE. Things will get better, and your dreams will manifest. Remember, you don't go through things—you GROW through things.

Out of everything I had lost, the most significant was my purpose. However, as the familiar saying goes, once you hit rock bottom, there's nowhere to go but up.

When I lost everything

Losing everything was a very humbling experience. My pride got in the way and prevented me from reaching out to family, so I didn't confide in them about what was going on. I had a few friends who knew my circumstances and offered me a spot to crash on their couch. There have been a few times on this dream journey that I've lost everything from going totally all-in. When I refer to losing everything, I mean being without money, shelter, and the means to feed myself. You might ask why I would put myself in such a position, right? The answer is this: because, at times, I have believed in myself and in my ability to prevail. I don't advise this for everyone. Depending on who you are and where you are in your journey, sometimes you have to burn ships so there is no return. I've taken calculated risks that did—or didn't—work out, and I also took with gut risks that did—or didn't—work. You have to do what's best for you.

I began to learn more about internet marketing; specifically, I learned about creating and selling physical and digital products. I begin to master my skills in this area, learning from the experts in this industry.

I began to invest in my spiritual and personal development and well-being. I began to serve others more. I doubled down on my skill sets and expertise and began to coach others more. I invested into obtaining knowledge and ways to constantly stay inspired and motivated.

What does this mean for you and your dreams? In order for someone to live their dreams out loud, they need to take the ideas, visions, and goals they think about every day and begin to act on them in everyday life. By finding clarity, taking care of my personal well-being, honing my gifts, committing to my goals, connecting with others, planning financially, and being disciplined, I was able to pull myself up from the valley and reach a peak I never thought possible. If you are reading this book, then I imagine, in some shape, you are seeking to do the same.

Your Origin Story

Everyone has a story. It's time you begin to craft yours!

Take a few minutes to consider where you came from and how that place, those people, and your experiences have shaped you. Consider these questions to get the ideas flowing.

- Where are you from?
- How has it shaped your life?
- What dreams did you have as a child?
- Have you fulfilled them?
- What pivot-point moments have made you who you are?
- How have they influenced you?

The Live Your Dreams Out Loud Commitment

The biggest challenge during the dream process is staying focused, disciplined, and committed to accomplishing your dreams, and this book is going to help you do exactly that. There will be days when you will not feel like Superman or Superwoman. You are human, but if you know how to stay committed—which you'll learn how to do—you will be able to shake those moments. At the end of the day, no matter how many books you read, how many programs you invest into, or how many mentors you have, it all starts and ends with you.

If you are unclear about the how it's going to happen, or if you are stuck on what it takes for you to succeed, this book will provide clarity. The unknown fear of the dream journey keeps people from discovering the true greatness that lies within them. If you are currently anything like I used to be, which is the epitome of being scattered, then you should begin to see a breakthrough after the first couple of chapters.

My commitment to succeed and not quit helped me see that sunshine was on the way, even in the midst of the darkest clouds. I somehow continued to dance in the rain despite the forecast. I committed myself to delivering the best content and experiences by turning them into tools for others to successfully achieve their dreams.

I am a firm believer that God kept me when I couldn't keep myself. This is not a book intended to promote my spiritual beliefs, but I have no reservations telling you that my faith and experiences all go back to God. Life's hurdles have been constant, yet through the grace of God, I somehow found a way to continue the race and jump over them.

You will get tired, you will mess up, you will feel stuck, you will feel as if no one understands, *blah, blah, blah...* Trust me, I have been there! Your commitment to your end goal of achieving your dream is more important than anything. Let's remember that.

I want you to sign this commitment to yourself so that if you don't take action, your signature is a reminder that every time you pick this book up, you aren't committed to yourself. On the flip side, I am confident that when you begin to achieve your dreams, you are going to look back and say, *"I committed myself."*

———————————

Are you ready to give up the excuses and commit to your dream, no matter what? If yes, what changes will you need to make immediately to honor this commitment? List them in the space provided.

_____

_____

_____

_____

_____

_____

_____

_____

_____

_____

_____

_____

I ,_____ , commit to taking action on my biggest goal in life: accomplishing my dream.

I know that my dream still has spark in it—the fact that I bought this book is all the evidence I need.

I will pursue this path with confidence.

I commit to implementing the strategies suggested in this book.

I will reflect on and answer all questions in the chapters ahead with honesty.

I promise to not give up on myself when detours pop up on my path.

As of today, _____ (date here),

I, _____ (name here), will begin to live my dreams out loud.

Signature _____

Date _____

Clarity

"Clarity of mind means clarity of passion, too;
this is why a great and clear mind loves ardently
and sees distinctly what he loves."

Blaise Pascal, mathematician

LIVE YOUR DREAMS OUT LOUD

Clarity and Quieting the Noise to Find Your Dream

- Get clear and gain perspective on what your biggest dreams truly are
- Clear your mind and focus on your passion and purpose
- Identify what you want from life
- Discover your inner motivator (or your "why")
- Learn how to overcome limiting beliefs and distractions

Do You Struggle With Focus?

If you're anything like I was (or anything like the dreamers I know and work with), you've struggled with a certain fear your whole life. I'm not referring to the typical fear of ridicule or of being unsuccessful. What I'm talking about is the fear of missing an opportunity.

Have you ever felt the urge to do as much as you can? To pursue every idea that pops into your head? To spread yourself too thin trying to do everything? I certainly have. As dreamers, many of us are prolific idea generators. Focusing in on just one thing can be the hardest thing we set our minds to do.

For many years, I've struggled between two loves: a passion for education and young people and a desire to help people through my own talk show, books, and speaking engagements. Given my excuses of limited resources and time, for many years, I didn't make any traction with my career as a thought leader because I was scattered. I finally decided to flip the switch and focus entirely on one thing at a time—and *that's* when the magic happened.

I'm guessing you've been there, too. Maybe you've felt that if you committed to one business idea, one career, one house, or one pathway, you would later regret it. I've learned the hard way that *indecision is still a decision*. By choosing too many things, you end up ruining your chances of succeeding at anything.

Managing Your Inner Visionary

Dreamers are visionaries. They may have a half-dozen ideas, images, or goals dancing around their heads at any moment. They may have tens of strategies to make these ideas happen. What's more, they could find an opportunity anywhere— they're constantly seeing ways to improve their world or pursue what's in their heart. As a result, many dreamers are driven *but distracted*.

Although the ability to generate ideas and solve problems quickly is a core component of our skill set as dreamers, it is also one of our greatest weaknesses. Chances are, we will burn ourselves out and see limited success if we don't cultivate the ability to focus and commit to one thing.

Imagine trying to play three basketball games at the same

time. No matter how athletic and gifted we might be, we would surely lose because we are not giving 100% to one game but tiring ourselves out trying to stretch ourselves between three.

How I gained clarity

I began to listen to my inner voice, and I formulated a plan based around those things that have always been important to me (living elsewhere in a more progressive place, enjoying entertainment, and having a job I enjoy).

I stopped thinking about compensation for a moment and started thinking about what I enjoyed most and really loved doing. I gained clarity and promised myself that I would one day work with the biggest celebrities in the entertainment business. Here's how I got clear about what I wanted most out of life:

1. Commitment
I knew I needed to commit, so I developed a strategy to help me get there. I left myself positive notes and reminders everywhere around the place that I was staying to ensure I was speaking my goals into existence as well as actively working on them every day.

2. Goals
I set short-, mid-, and long-term goals (those tangible steps) for myself. I put them on a timeline of three, six, and nine months.

My short-term goal was to establish accountability partners, so I put together a team of like-minded, forward-thinking friends who could check in with me on my progress. My mid-term goal was to identify and seek out a mentor, someone whose success I admired, could learn from, and potentially pattern my career after. My third and final goal, which really had been on-going this entire time, was to raise and save enough money to cover my basic needs so I could focus all my time and energy on my dream.

3. Focus

Even after committing to these goals I'd set for myself, I still struggled with various distractions in my life. I had to ask myself, "What are the things I am currently holding on to that are standing in the way my success?" I made a list of all of my distractions and bad habits and began to prioritize letting those things go. This was by no means a painless process, and a process indeed it was. I had to give myself time and understanding yet remain firm and disciplined. My dream became the North Star that always led me back to the right path when I had gone astray.

4. Action

I could dream, scheme, and plan all I wanted, but until I put one foot in front of the other, none of it mattered. I set these goals, I acted on these goals, and I stuck to these goals. **THAT** is the essence of Living Your Dreams Out Loud.

Your yellow brick path to gaining clarity

Dorothy needed to follow a yellow brick road to accomplish her destiny. Similarly, there is a 5-step "yellow brick road" to understanding, planning for, and executing your dream with clarity.

Step 1: Shun Indecision

Learn to be decisive, especially concerning your dream. For a season, stop saying things like, "Whatever you'd prefer." Make choices and stop handing the reins of your life over to other people.

Our culture often labels decisive people as rude. As a result, there's a bias against being decisive in our daily lives. From something as simple as what you eat for breakfast to where you get after-work drinks, the habit of passing decisions onto others is commonplace and crippling.

If you are serious about living your dreams, you need to become serious about making decisions. Some dreamers don't learn to make decisions, and they spend most of their lives passing their choices to others. Dreamers destined to become dream-livers cultivate the ability to make and stick with hard choices.

PUT IT INTO PRACTICE

This week, don't delegate a single decision, no matter how small. Focus on making every choice concerning

*your life by yourself (from where and what you eat
to what brand of laundry detergent you buy). Just for
this week, look for your own facts and make your own
choices quickly and definitively.*

Step 2: Commit to a Vision for Your Future

Take some time to imagine the future you want. Write down what you see, or if possible, lay it out visually on a vision board. Commit to this singular vision of your future. Promise yourself you won't stop until you get there.

A handful of studies over the past fifty years have proven that individuals who write down and commit to goals accomplish much more than their peers. In fact, the more specific the vision and goals a person has and the more clearly those goals are expressed, the more they will have accomplished.

PUT IT INTO PRACTICE

*Stop discussing your dream in generalities; get really,
really specific. What exactly do you want your dream
to look like? How will you be spending your days?
What will you be doing? Write it down and spend time
reading your vision every day, even if only for a few
minutes. Use it as the measuring stick for the decisions
you're making: are they supporting your vision or not?*

Step 3: Set Concrete Long-Term, Medium-Term, and Short-Term Goals

Now that you've committed to a vision for your future, the next step is to map the path to get there and to lay it out on paper. At this step, you won't be choosing the specific strategies you'll use (that comes later). You'll simply be marking the bite-sized milestones that signify progress toward your dream. These milestones should be specific and significant indicators that you are well on your way to achieving your dream. What are the steps to get there? In two years, what should you have accomplished? In one year? In six months?

PUT IT INTO PRACTICE

Set five or six specific goals that are benchmarks on the way to living your dream out loud. Try to space the goals so some can be carried out within six months, some within one year, and some within two years. Put these goals up somewhere prominent, so you can revisit them often.

Step 4: Make These Goals Your North Star

Your goals are the backbone to the future you want. If you aim for them and reach them within your set timeline, your vision will happen! So now, you need to relentlessly align your life to these goals; make them your North Star—your guiding focus as you make lifestyle choices. This is especially true of how you prioritize your time and financial resources. Until you carry out your dream, your discretionary time and resources need to go to activities that will get you closer to those goals. Cut out every distraction that doesn't move you toward these goals.

PUT IT INTO PRACTICE

Make a stop-doing list. Monitor your activities and relentlessly cut back on things that move you away from the goals you've set. Be prepared for backlash; some people may not understand why you don't do some of the things you used to do. Be confident; as long as you're focusing on activities aligned with your North Star, you will get the results you want!

Step 5: Act

Now that you know what you're aiming for, taking focused, strategic action to get there. The best goals and the most iron-clad "stop doing" list in the world can't make your dreams come true. That's because in addition to planning to act, you need to act. Become the person you dream of being.

PUT IT INTO PRACTICE

Make a list of steps you will take in the next thirty days to move your dream forward. Revisit that list every month and cross out completed items (and add new ones as your benchmarks change). Become a person of action, and your dreams will come into view sooner than you imagine.

Find Your "Sweet-Spot" of Value

> "Accept no one's definition of your life, but define yourself."
>
> Harvey Fierstein

The journey to clarity involves some questions for reflection:
- What is your gift *to the world*?
- What unique value do you bring?
- What problem do your skills and talents answer?
- What makes you happy?
- What ignites your passions?

These may be questions you've heard before but have struggled to answer for a while.

I'm here to tell you that until you have a compelling answer to this question, you will be trapped in an unfulfilled life. For most of us, life will not get better until we get clear on what we want and demand out of life. This journey begins when we figure out what life wants out of us.

I, along with countless others, have learned this lesson the hard way. I'm authoring this book so you won't have to.

The good news is, once you get clear on what you want and focused on how to get it, every failure or setback becomes a tool you can use to propel you forward. Every win becomes gasoline on the fire to accelerate you toward you purpose.

———————————

What unique gift, talent, solution, or idea do people need that you can provide?

_____

_____

_____

_____

_____

What need does this gift, talent, solution, or idea address?

_____

_____

_____

_____

_____

THE GREATER THE
OBSTACLE
the **GLORY**
more
IN OVERCOMING IT.

AIM for the Life You Want

"Desire is the starting point of all achievement, not a hope, not a wish, but a keen pulsating desire which transcends everything."

Napoleon Hill

Once you know what your gift to the world is, it's time to focus in on what you want to do with your life. For some people, this is as traditional as finding a mate and getting married. For others, it's starting a business or launching a product. It can all feel overwhelming and frightening. Regardless of what your end goal is and how much it will change over time, you need to have a goal you're committed to right now as a starting place to begin moving forward.

This is your line in the sand—a uniting principle—that will motivate you when all hell is breaking loose where your dreams are concerned.

No SMART Goals Needed

By now, many of you may have heard of "SMART" goals. In case you haven't, the SMART acronym stands for Specific, Measurable, Achievable, Relevant and Time-bound. It's a popular concept, but when it comes to your dreams, a SMART goal is your worst enemy.

Here's why: SMART goals are goals designed to help you make incremental progress. They include goals that are "realistic" (also known as low-ball or beneath your potential). As a dreamer, goals that are inherently realistic are also often demotivating. Until your life's goal exhilarates you, you won't be powerful enough to bust through your own fears, habits, and the undertow of complacency that attacks all of us. SMART goals are for status quo individuals; dreamers need ambitious AIMs, not SMART goals.

With that in mind, we are going to work with a different acronym called AIM.

An AIM is a Goal That Is:

Authentic: real to you and consistent with your beliefs and values, and a gift to the world.
Intimidating: bigger than you can do on your own.
Motivating: so exciting and meaningful to you, it compels you to move forward.

Moving forward

"The greater the obstacle, the more glory in overcoming it."
Moliere

Now that you've decided what your gift to the world is, and now that you have set some concrete AIMs for your life, it's time to make a plan to move forward.

It's one thing to have good intentions; it's another to make and execute a fool-proof plan to your success. What stands between you and your dream begins with clarity about what obstacles you'll have to overcome in order to meet success. This is a place where many dreamers miss the mark.

How many entrepreneurs have you met had a grand vision but then—because they didn't plan for obstacles—lost sight of their dream? Whether the obstacle is the cost of doing business, the impact of market forces on business, or a myriad of other challenges, choosing to ignore or dismiss challenges in order to move forward is a mistake.

A common objection to this principle is that predicting obstacles or challenges is a "negative" activity that will make us fearful about our future. Let's be real: many of us are fearful anyway. By anticipating and naming those things we're concerned about, we can put together a plan to overcome them. By hiding from them, we make it even more likely that we will experience them.

Dreamer Spotlight: Howard Hughes and the Dangers of AIM-less Living

If anyone in the world was set up to be successful from day one, it was Howard Hughes. Not only was he born into a wealthy, prestigious family, but he was also a mechanical and engineering prodigy. He was so skilled at mathematics and mechanical pursuits that he built Houston's first transmitter at only eleven years old, his own mechanical bicycle at twelve, and broke several world records at an early age. If anyone had the talent to be a true winner in life, it was Hughes.

When his mother and father died, Hughes inherited 75% of his father's business along with his fortune...and that's when the trouble began. From his earliest adult years, Hughes suffered from an unwillingness to focus on any one endeavor for any length of time. He allowed himself to become distracted perpetually. Hughes made a series of impulsive, wasteful choices that began to destroy his life. His quick success in a myriad of industries led him to begin to take on projects that he didn't have the capacity to perform. Over the next twenty years, he would design, fly, and crash two faulty airplanes that cost his business (and the U.S. government) millions of dollars. These accidents devastated his body, causing his last two decades of life to be riddled with physical pain. His unwillingness to commit to a single woman led to two divorces and many failed relationships.

Although Hughes had almost unlimited resources and natural ability, he ended his life in obscurity because he was never really sure about what he wanted. By choosing to have everything, he ended up with nothing.

We've all heard of stories of professional athletes, actors, or others losing big by trying their hand at an industry or project that was outside their core focus area. Avoid their mistake by deciding what you want and going after it with all your might.

Your turn: Defining your dreams

Name your dream AIM here:

_____

_____

_____

_____

_____

_____

_____

_____

_____

What other desires will you need to put on hold to pursue
your dream?

_____

_____

_____

_____

_____

What challenges do you foresee on the path to pursuing
your dream?

_____

_____

_____

_____

_____

What strategies can you use to overcome these obstacles
and challenges?

_____

_____

_____

_____

_____

What can you do to keep yourself focused when other opportunities come your way?

_____

_____

_____

_____

_____

Free training video

Before you proceed visit the link below.

www.LiveYourDreamsOutLoud.com/book-clarity

Commitment

"Unless commitment is made, there are only promises and hopes… but no plans."

Peter Drucker, writer and philosopher

Chapter 2:

Commitment and Owning Your Dream

- Define commitment
- Find solutions to obstacles
- Overcome complacency
- Confront your fears

Knowing your dream, and developing the needed skills to achieve that dream, is just the beginning. In order to accelerate your progress and go from dreaming to doing, you need to have commitment . You need to stop renting your dream and start owning it. Now that you're clear, you must become invested in making your dream happen at almost any cost.

One of my greatest revelations in pursuing my dream was how much commitment it really took to be successful. We see these stories of successful thought leaders, athletes, and performers and think their talent alone earned them their success. The truth is, the journey is usually painful, fraught with disappointments and struggle, and in need of all the commitment you can muster.

The hero of this story isn't me.

I grew up with a mother who refused to give up on finding a way as a single parent. She worked three, sometimes four jobs and still struggled to make ends meet. She endured hardships, frustrations, the constant worry of struggling for money, but she still kept fighting. She let my brother and I know from a very young age that we would have to aggressively pursue what we needed to survive. It became clear to me—based on her actions of commitment—that her dream was to provide us with everything she didn't have in order for us to have the best life possible.

One day, when I was fairly young, my mom put us to bed and gathered up all her bills. Although I was supposed to be asleep, I watched her spread the bills out like a blanket over our dining room table. Then, I saw her scribble in a notepad, listing each of the bills and adding up the total. When the numbers wouldn't add up, I saw her tear up. Seeing my mom struggle and being unable to help was one of the pivotal experiences of my life. In fact, my hustle and desire to be an entrepreneur was born out of that moment.

The bags under my mom's eyes from trying to put food on the table taught my brother and I that you don't make excuses for why things are as they are: you find a solution.

Even though several colleges recruited me to play basketball, I didn't receive a scholarship, and that's when my mother's commitment took center stage. Rather than discourage me or advise me to choose a lesser school, she drove me to a half-dozen colleges to try out for their teams in person. Her commitment to me, even when circumstances looked bleak, proved to me that she believed I had what it took to secure a college scholarship, and I did just that. Her actions taught me that commitment to someone or something requires sacrifice, and sometimes that sacrifice defies logic.

YOU NEED TO STOP RENTING YOUR DREAM *and* START OWNING IT.

She was there for me at one of the toughest moments of my life, when I almost gave up my future. I now know that the seeds of commitment she planted on the inside of me helped me to rebuild after that dark moment. Her willingness to fight and keep on fighting proved to me that there was no "quit" in me because there was no "quit" in her. I realize now that one of the reasons I always bounced back from disappointments was because my mother's resilience and stalwart commitment to me left a lasting imprint on my heart. I love you, Mom!

It took everything I had to make it to my dream—real commitment to my outcome, regardless of what I had to go through to get there. It will require the same of you.

Declaring War on Your Own Complacency

Everyone knows that renting something feels different than buying or owning it. That's why so many apartment renters never paint the walls of their homes, but many new home-owners paint their houses before even moving in. That's why we fill rental cars up with the cheapest gasoline we can find but put premium gas in our newly-purchased vehicles. When it comes to our dreams, that's why we spend months or even years in a holding pattern, renting and waiting for the most convenient time to act rather than making the sacrifices we know will make the biggest difference.

The first step to truly owning your dream is to no longer accept being a mediocre, barely-committed hobbyist where your dream is concerned. Complacency and becoming comfortable with a low-risk, average life is your enemy.

When it comes to complacency in your life, my orders are simple: terminate it with extreme prejudice.

How do you figure out what's causing the complacency in your life? It's simple: it comes down to the behaviors, habits, and hobbies that currently dictate your life. If you can figure out the handful of things you are doing, or that you should be doing, and make the necessary adjustments, you will destroy complacency. More importantly, you will become a dream-catcher, not just a dream-chaser.

Confidence in the Face of Challenges

A lack of commitment is usually caused by one of two things: a fear of sacrifice (what it will cost to commit to something) or a fear that what you devote yourself to will fail. In the case of the latter, it usually sounds something like this, "I would find a new job, but…" (completing the sentence with a statement that reveals a fear of failure).

People who own their dreams believe in their power to overcome challenges. They remember the challenges they and others have been victorious over, and they use those challenges as fodder to move forward when times get hard. They don't overestimate their abilities, but they know that when they give themselves wholeheartedly to confronting a challenge, they usually win.

In our culture, we're often told that our "average"

accomplishments aren't significant. Holding our own against an abusive boss or enduring a messy divorce seems to pale in comparison with Lance Armstrong's Tour De France victory. It seems almost silly to brag about these things, to ourselves, or even to others. As a result, when most driven, accomplished people think of their accomplishments, they're often over-whelmed with the anxious feeling that they aren't excelling fast enough.

Successful dreamers, on the other hand, focus on what they have accomplished—not to become complacent, but as proof that they have a track record of overcoming obstacles. They know their history and expect their trend of succeeding to continue, as long as they put in the work.

Confronting Your Fear of Suffering for Your Dream

As I mentioned earlier, a fear of sacrifice or suffering for your dream can be a significant challenge to your commitment level. As someone who's battled this first-hand, I know how challenging it can be to both...

1. Admit that you're unwilling to give up certain things for your dream.
2. Admit that you're scared of the process you'll have to go through to make it happen.

Most people don't find inspiration in hearing about how a strug-gling actor lived in their car for two years before they hit it big;

the price of their commitment sends a shiver up people's spines.

The good news is, you can avoid the unnecessary suffering some new dreamers experience when they step out too early or without the right preparation.

Some of the horror stories we hear could have been mitigated or avoided altogether with the first two steps of our Live Your Dreams Out Loud journey. This doesn't mean that our dreams won't cost us; it just means that by building out the process, step by step, we will avoid unnecessary struggles and accelerate toward our desired goal.

You and I both know that anything in life worth pursuing costs something. In fact, it's often the case that the more it costs us, the greater the potential reward can be. Think about childbirth: the discomfort of a woman carrying a child in her womb for nine months and the hours of agony required to give birth to that child. Who in their right mind would pursue that? Millions of women each year persevere through the birthing process because of the great reward at the end of their journeys.

How about getting a college degree? Anyone who's graduated from college, particularly those at a top-tier college or with a challenging course of study, know that although college is fun, it's not all fun and games. Masters degrees are even more challenging. Think about it: why would we pay ridiculous prices for these degrees, and put in years of more effort, and forgo thousands of dollars in a salary to go back to school full-time for two years? It's simple: because we believe the process is going to prepare us for the future we want. And that, my friends, is the secret to overcoming the fear of sacrifice: having confidence that the process we are engaged in will propel us to the life we want. If we aren't confident in the process, we won't be able to dig deep and make the right choices, consistently, to get us to our goals.

You need to decide that no matter what comes that you will not allow yourself to give up or fail. Failure is when you quit. If you can't fully commit to that today, put the book down until you're ready to fully commit. Here's why: fate and providence favor the committed. Until you've deeply committed and are willing to pay the needed price for what you want, you're stuck in a holding pattern.

Having lots of information won't profit you in a holding pattern. In fact, it will only frustrate you, because you'll see people less skilled and less knowledgeable going farther and faster than you.

Dreamer Spotlight: Jaime Escalante and Confronting Challenges to Succeed

Jaime Escalante was a Bolivian immigrant in his late thirties who had spent a dozen years teaching math in his native country. Because of certification requirements, he was unable to teach in the U.S. before earning a separate university degree and taking a handful of classes to master the English language. Instead, this seasoned teacher took on odd jobs while he earned the needed prerequisites to get back in the classroom.

At the age of 44, he finally earned the degrees he needed to return to the classroom. He got a job at Garfield High School (one of the most dangerous and chronically underperforming high schools in Los Angeles). His students were so far behind that he was on the brink of quitting, and that's when he found twelve students willing to take an algebra class.

Jaime believed that rather than lowering expectations, Garfield should require their students to take harder math courses, even calculus. His philosophy was so controversial it almost got him fired a handful of times in his first four years at Garfield. Then, in 1978, he got his big break: the chance to teach one section of AP calculus to a group of five students. Although no one believed even one student would pass the AP calculus test, two students passed. The next year, nine students took the class and seven passed. Within four years, the class size had ballooned to fifteen students, fourteen of whom passed the AP calculus test. Jaime's class came under scrutiny when eighteen students passed the AP test in one year. The Educational Testing Service performed thorough investigations; they even required students to re-take the AP test, as if they'd cheated the first time.

Remarkably, this persecution only made Jaime's resolve stronger. He continued to expand the math program and willingly overpopulated classes so more students could take his advanced math. President Ronald Reagan even commended Escalante for his hard work and dedication to teaching math. The film Stand and Deliver memorializes his story.

By refusing to give up on his dream, Jaime encouraged thousands of California students to pursue degrees and careers in science, technology, engineering, and math.

Your turn: taking action

Where are you most stagnant or complacent in your dreamer journey?

_____

_____

_____

_____

_____

What behaviors, habits, or hobbies might be contributing to your stagnancy or complacency?

_____

_____

_____

_____

_____

Highlight or circle the behavior, habit, or hobby that has become the biggest hindrance to your dream that you named above.

What is one step you can commit to in the next 24 hours to terminate this behavior with extreme prejudice?

_____

_____

_____

_____

_____

In what areas of your life have you experienced the biggest setbacks?

_____

_____

_____

_____

_____

What are some things you can do or skills you can develop to come back stronger from those weaknesses or defeats?

_____

_____

_____

_____

_____

What challenges are you most concerned about related to your dream? Why?

_____

_____

_____

_____

_____

What challenges have you already overcome in your life? What have those challenges shown about your character and resilience?

_____

_____

_____

_____

_____

How can you use your history to give you the courage to confront these challenges head-on?

_____

_____

_____

_____

_____

Have you ever lowered your goals or dreams because the challenges you faced seemed too great? When?

_____

_____

_____

_____

_____

Tell the truth: What are you afraid of having to give up in order to pursue your dream?

_____

_____

_____

_____

_____

When you think about the process of walking out your dream, what piece of the process scares you the most?

_____

_____

_____

_____

_____

Wht are some ways you could prepare now for unexpected challenges to your dream?

_____

_____

_____

_____

_____

Free Training Video

Before you proceed visit the link below.

www.LiveYourDreamsOutLoud.com/book-Commitment

Connections

"A dream you dream alone is only a dream.
A dream you dream together is reality."

John Lennon

Master the Art of Connections

- Value your own skills and experiences
- Understand the practical to-dos of networking
- Master the art of making friends
- Learn how to find mentors
- Partner with allies to support your dreams

More than any other skill, the ability to connect with people has been my secret weapon in my arduous pursuit of living out my dream. In addition to winning over mentors and sponsors, the ability to connect with others has helped me to make the most of every opportunity. You never know how a connection today can help you tomorrow.

Why Forming and Maintaining Relationships Matters

"No man is an island."
"It takes a village to raise a child."
"When it comes to success, there are no lone rangers."
You might be thinking that you've heard these phrases

before, on repeat, ad nauseam. I'd heard them, too, and they never really stuck with me until I started living out loud and applying those old, sage adages to my daily life. I now know that far too many dreamers fail on the path to pursuing their future because they try to go it alone. There are plenty of reasons why this happens, but they generally fall into four categories:

1. A fear that by networking you are becoming a selfish, schmoozing, opportunistic hustler (or being perceived as one)
2. Fear and confusion about how networking happens and where to go to meet the people you want to reach out to
3. Missing out on opportunities when they arise due to poor planning or lack of follow-up
4. Remaining in unfruitful but familiar personal relationships, rather than upgrading your friendships to suit your future goals

I learned pretty early how important relationships are. As a young entrepreneur, people were the lifeline of my business. Starting at six years old, I sold pencils. Then I moved on to giving haircuts to people in the community, knocking on doors to cut grass, washing cars—the list goes on. I learned that if people didn't like or trust me, they wouldn't buy anything from me; learning that lesson at a young age was critical. In high school and college, this skillset helped me form relationships with many of my teachers, some of whom became my mentors and supporters. In my senior year of high school, those relationships gave me the recommendations, encouragement, and advice I needed to secure a college basketball scholarship after multiple failed attempts.

When I decided to live my dreams out loud, it dawned on me that I needed to find someone who had been successful at what I was trying to achieve and to learn from them directly. As an adult, my ability to connect with others has led to some of the greatest professional accomplishments of my life.

Why are we afraid to network?

Human beings are inherently social creatures. We live in communities. We marry. We learn in communities. So, why is the process of reaching out to others who know more than we do so nerve-racking?

Part of the reason networking makes many dreamers uncomfortable is because in the past, unskilled networkers have used aggressive, selfish, and unethical tactics in order to further their own aims. With the internet, these tactics have become even more prevalent. As a result, customers, potential allies, and others are on the defensive. In our mind, no matter what we say, or how valuable our proposition is, we believe our intended connection will think we're a fraud.

Here's the problem with this way of thinking: it assumes that the exchange in a networking relationship is always one-sided. This couldn't be further from the truth. When real networking happens, both parties benefit and move forward toward their desired outcome. To do this kind of value-added networking, you need to radically shift how you view yourself and the value you bring to the table. Until that happens, you're going to be trapped in a "salesman-with-their-hand-out" mentality. Nothing repels potential partners, clients, or mentors more than a person acting like a bad used car salesman.

How making connections changed my life

In December 2008, I was given an opportunity to consult for a non-profit organization as a project manager when I first started my consulting business. Little did I know that a job posting for a consultant on Craigslist would be instrumental to the connections that would help open up doors for the rest of my life.

I didn't have the experience on paper that the job called for (eight-ten years of project management experience), but the executive director and I were members of the same fraternity, and he wanted to give me a chance. I was committed to getting this nonprofit as my first client, and sure enough, after six months of going back and forth, he told me that another fraternity brother had given him an opportunity similar to this when he was younger and that he wanted to do the same for me. His exact words were, "Consider this one on the shield and pay it forward," which meant that he wanted to grant me an opportunity not only because of my relentless pursuit and ability to do the job but to continue carrying out the true definition of fraternity and brotherhood. I needed to continue passing the baton. Having that connection and this guy as my mentor until this day has been one of the best connections ever.

IN ORDER TO ACCOMPLISH
YOUR DREAM, YOU NEED TO BUILD
MORE THAN JUST A NETWORK,

you need an

ECOSYSTEM OF PEOPLE

WHO ARE ALIGNED TO YOU,
YOUR ECOSYSTEM,
YOUR IDEAS AND YOUR CAUSE.

You may not have been part of a college fraternity or sorority, but there have certainly been other groups or smaller communities that you've been a member of at some time or another. Any of the following places are places that can be a network for you to tap into:

- A team or club you were once a member of
- Your gym/fitness center
- Your house of worship
- You group of friends
- Your family
- The coffee shop or bar you frequent
- Social media networks like Instagram, Facebook, or Pinterest
- Professional networks like your local chamber of commerce, an association, or LinkedIn

In December 2010, I had one of these make-it-or-break-it moments. I was given the unique opportunity to attend a business dinner at Mr. Chow's in Beverly Hills with talk show host and author Tavis Smiley and music executive, entrepreneur, and film producer Clarence Avant. I had met Clarence while I was consulting for a client in Atlanta. Clarence and I had begun to build a relationship based on our way of joking with one another (we were both from small country towns). I'd followed Tavis for some time but had never met him face-to-face. My fraternity brother's father was a former business associate of Tavis and had always provided me with books written by Tavis.

The purpose of the dinner meeting was pretty straight-forward: booking Tavis to be the emcee at a conference at

University of Southern California for my client. Clarence Avant served on the advisory board for my client at the time. He was taking the lead to get Tavis to emcee the event, and I was there to close the deal. During our conversation, I discovered that Tavis and I had a lot in common. He also grew up in the South in a single-parent home and in a trailer, had a challenging upbringing, went to a prestigious college, and moved to LA to pursue his dreams of being a thought leader. These similarities and my immense respect for his work combined to lead me to taking a risk: I decided to offer to volunteer or help him if the opportunity ever arose. He responded in kind, giving me the "if you ever need anything" card.

Although there were several occasions where I thought of cashing in on this offer after the meeting, I sat on the card for a while. I did this for two reasons: I wanted to make sure I had a concrete reason to reach out to him, and I wanted to make sure that whatever I asked for would add a lot of value to him and his business as well.

Several years later, I was in a desperate place on my dream journey. I'd experienced several crushing setbacks, one on the heels of another. I knew I needed inspiration—and fast. It just so happened that Tavis and Dr. Cornel West were scheduled to speak in Atlanta at the same time. At the time, I had finished my educational pilot project with the students and had gotten confirmation that my purpose of being a thought leader was brewing in my spirit at an all-time high. It was time for me to explore the path of producing and hosting an inspirational show of my own.

It dawned on me that I needed to find someone who had been successful at what I was trying to achieve and to learn from them directly. That day, after his speech, I spoke with Tavis and asked him for a conference call to discuss some things related to my career.

After the event, I went home and formulated an email proposal to Tavis about my career plan and decided to "cash in on the card." Tavis had his team set up a conference call with me a few weeks after the email proposal. A few weeks passed, and I was in Orlando with my friend Wayne Anderson. I needed to get out of Atlanta to re-shift my energy as I was awaiting this call from Tavis. My pitch to Tavis was specific: to come shadow him for a few months while helping him in any area in his business.

Initially, my plan was to shadow Tavis while positioning and developing my own brand, but two weeks prior to my move, an opportunity opened up that I couldn't refuse. Tavis called and said that his event producer was leaving and if interested, could I produce his national televised event that was going to take place the weekend of the 2012 presidential inauguration in Washington DC. The opportunity was unpaid, and it was the chance of a lifetime for me. I took it and never looked back.

I didn't know how I would move to LA without any money, but I just trusted my gut and had faith that this was the right thing to do. Thanks to good friends and a generous offer from Tavis to sponsor my lodging, I was well on my way to finding the career success and satisfaction I was longing for and—more importantly—I made a friend and mentor for life.

I can't emphasize enough how important it is to reduce your learning curve by learning from others who have mastered the desired dream of yours. My sole intent, when given the opportunity to work amongst some of the greatest to ever do it, was to learn and study the how.

Building an Out Loud Community

Even with these amazing moments and the rare opportunities that followed, the flow has almost always been the same: truly connecting with someone else, finding ways to help them, and being open to opportunities to partner when they arise.

In order to accomplish your dream, you need to build more than just a network: you need an ecosystem of people who align to you, your ideas, and your cause. Not all these individuals will be in your inner circle (most won't be). Instead, you'll be building a community of friends who support you and who you support: the kind of community that makes everyone better.

Your cheerleaders (people who unconditionally believe in your abilities; committed fans)

These individuals don't have the skills or experiences to help you make good decisions concerning your dreams, but they cheer you on from the stands.

Chances are, in your family and friends circle alone, you have access to one or two truly consistent cheerleaders. These individuals believe in you unconditionally and have no doubt you will accomplish whatever you put your mind to. They keep you encouraged and motivated on your dream journey.

Enjoy their company and reciprocate their unfeigned

support as they pursue their dreams, but be careful not to ask cheerleaders for advice. Although they'd never knowingly steer you wrong, they may not have the experience or expertise to help you make the best choices concerning your dreams.

Your mastermind (a group of peers skilled in various areas who can advise you on specific areas concerning your dream and call you out for your weak thinking, negative attitude, or slack-off behavior concerning your dream)

Your mastermind group is the people you see as your true professional peers and colleagues. This select group represents the people in your life who share your drive and passion but are achieving success in a different context than you are. Together, your joint expertise forms a mastermind: a bank of knowledge the community can pull on as you each move forward.

This group's intention is not to be your greatest cheerleaders. In fact, sometimes it is the role of a mastermind to call you out on unrealistic ideas or weak behavior. It's a mistake to assume your mastermind will behave as "yes men." That's not their job, nor should it be.

Your direct mentors (individuals further along on their dream journey who've agreed to mentor you directly via one-on-one conversations, phone calls, emails, or feedback on your ideas; paid coaches can also be direct mentors)

Your direct mentors are the handful of accomplished individuals in your life who are committed to developing you personally and professionally. This select group is made of individuals who each have a specific area of expertise to contribute to you professionally or personally. You give richly into these individuals, both with your time and labor but also financially or with gifts as appropriate.

These individuals have their own busy, accomplished lives to lead, so you must be considerate and low-maintenance as a mentee. Don't waste their time; be prepared and thoughtful before you ask them for anything.

Your indirect mentors (thought leaders and dreamers whose lives and wisdom you glean from, either through books, interviews, courses, or other passive sources of information)

Your indirect mentors are the larger group of thought leaders, dreamers, and exceptional individuals whose stories and insights move you toward your dreams. You follow these individuals by reading their material and interviews and learning from their lives.

Having indirect mentors isn't enough. You need real people in your life to cheer you on and to hold you accountable for reaching your dreams.

Your mentees (individuals looking to you for support, guidance, and inspiration; their success further solidifies your success)

Your mentees are the handful of individuals you take under your wing and help to move toward their goals. As you see them succeed, their success is further proof of the value you bring and the skills you possess.

Establish clear boundaries with your mentees and protect your time. Although you should be eager to help them advance, be careful not to do the hard work for them. Set time and productivity expectations for your mentees; if they don't meet them, don't let them waste your time.

Your allies (connections you make who contribute to your dream for seasons or with time-bound and/or infrequent support)

Your allies are the individuals and organizations you meet along the journey that support you or your cause but **aren't directly connected** to you in a deep way. These individuals and organizations often offer time-bound, strategic support when you need it.

Generosity is the key to cultivating allies. Offer to support them as they reach their goals and they will support you as you reach yours.

~~~~~~~~

Sean "P. Diddy" Combs: A Case Study in Cultivating Allies to Reach Business Success

Hip-hop and business mogul Sean "P. Diddy" Combs was born in a housing project in Harlem, N.Y. His father was a drug dealer who was gunned down when Combs was small, and his mother struggled to make ends meet working as a teacher's aide and a model. After graduating from high school, Combs entered Howard University to major in business, but he dropped out of college before earning a B.A. degree and began an internship at Uptown Records.

Combs excelled at attracting and forming relationships with rising talent. During his time at Uptown Records, he developed the talent of rising stars like Mary J. Blige and Jodeci. He also managed to throw exceptionally wild parties, some attracting as many as one thousand guests. This was because everyone knew Combs, the young talent director at Uptown Records.

Later on, Combs partnered with Clive Davis—a contact he'd made earlier in his career—to launch Bad Boy Records. It is rumored that Davis invested $1.5 million in this project, funds the young music exec needed to get the fledgling record company off the ground. Although Combs was a master at producing hit records, his true gift was identifying, cultivating, and building meaningful relationships with diamonds in the rough—talented artists who were stronger as a portfolio than they were individually. Soon after Combs helped Christopher "Biggie" Wallace produce his first top-selling album, Combs brought on a dozen other show-stopping new talents.

Even though Combs' life took a series of dips, his financial prowess and expansive network allowed him to surround himself with wise and powerful people, to rebrand, and to move forward. He exemplifies what it means to have a broad ecosystem of allies across your sector (and even in other industries) in order to reach your professional goals.

Combs knows *everyone that matters* in his industries. How would you assess the value of the network you have? Are there any A-listers in your network? What can you do to upgrade your network of allies over the next 3 months?

A Crash Course in Building Your Network

In terms of connecting with others, finding the right mentor(s) is one of highest-value activities an up-and-coming dreamer can engage in. It's also one of the most challenging activities, because so few people take the time to tell you *how* to build a strong network.

As you mature in your craft and industry, you'll develop your own flair for networking. Until then, here's a 5-step approach to get you there:

Step 1: Optimize Your Social Media

Before you kick your networking into overdrive, ensure your social media profiles are complete and convey the information you want them to. There's nothing worse than building a pipeline of new potential partners, only for them to find a questionable Facebook picture or a half-complete LinkedIn account.

Make sure your Instagram profile is up to date and that your bio is a reflection of your work. **Instead of just scrolling down the Instagram timeline, update your profile to a business profile and begin to look at the analytics of your content. Search hashtags that are aligned with your mission.**

At the very least, you need to edit your Facebook account. Make sure your Facebook name is appropriate and professional. Don't post any questionable content, photos, or affiliations (and remove any that might already be there).

Make sure your privacy settings don't allow strangers to view things you don't want them to see.

Next, complete a professional profile on LinkedIn that includes a photo, accurate work history, and any relevant qualifications. Ensure your LinkedIn URL matches your name (e.g. www.LinkedIn.com/in/JohnSmith).

You can create a Twitter account or Pinterest account if appropriate, but only if you plan to update it consistently. Ensure that the tweets and posts in cyberspace reflect what you want someone to see if they google you.

Step Two: Make a prioritized list of contacts

Research and write down the important names in your industry or sector. Make sure to include headliners, as well as the people on the ground doing the work or any rising talent.

Create three lists to organize the contacts by their degree of accomplishment in your field. In Tier 1, you might have Beyoncé. Tier 2 might be her manager, and Tier 3 might be the head of the studio where she dances. Keep in mind that, early on in your journey, Tier 2 and 3 contacts will likely be of more value to you than Tier 1 contacts (and they will definitely be more accessible). For example, if you are still trying to improve your vocal range and have yet to master your craft, P. Diddy is not the right person to focus on, but a well-known vocal coach might be.

Across these lists, star the top five names you are committed to connecting with in a meaningful way this year. Choose these names based on their degree of usefulness at this point in your dream journey, their perceived accessibility (how easy it will be to connect with them) and their reputation/level of access in your industry.

Step Three: Put Together a Plan

Put together a tactical plan for reaching out to these five people. This might include attending conferences where they're likely to be, using LinkedIn to see if you share a mutual contact, joining LinkedIn groups they're also a part of, or using Twitter to retweet posts they've released or to direct message them.

The important thing is that you should stagger your plan and ensure that it's thorough (and don't be sketchy—you don't want to be confused for a stalker!). Don't attempt fifty contact strategies on the same day; pace yourself over time.

There are several great books to help you in the planning phase: Never Eat Alone by Keith Ferrazzi, for example, includes detailed information about putting your plan together.

Step Four: Execute Your Plan

Add deadlines to your plan and begin to execute it. Along the way, expect to find additional opportunities to grow your network. As you put the work in, more chances will open up. Be sure to front-load (adding value) to people whenever possible. This makes the relationship more organic and valuable for both parties and makes the connections you are forming even stronger.

Step Five: Put a Communication System in Place to Keep Your Network Alive

Only two words separate mediocre networkers from master networkers: artful follow-up. The truth is, making a powerful first impression is really important. With that said, once that short conversation is over, even the most well-meaning ally will forget you, unless you follow up well.

You can create your own custom follow-up system over time, but here's a tried-and-true follow-up system you can use right now:

- **Collect annotated business cards**. Shortly after someone hands you a business card, write down key details (how you can help them, how they can help you, what follow-up you promised) on the back of their business card. Collect business cards in the back of your business card holder. Transcribe them into a spreadsheet or other system within 24 hours.
- **Send a follow-up email within 48 hours, detailing who you are, how you can help them, and any action steps they agreed to in your conversation.** This email should be concise and professional and end with a concrete ask, such as the following:
  - » "Let's check in for 15 minutes sometime in the next few weeks. Here are the best three times for me. [list dates/times]. I look forward to hearing from you about when works best for our check in."
  - » "Thanks for offering to connect me to [person's name]. I'd be happy to draft an email for you, or to

reach out myself and include your name. Please let me know what I can do to help make this happen."

» "Thanks for sending me [specific information]. As I mentioned, it will be a huge help as I undertake [x activity], so thanks again for sending it along. In the meantime, here's an [article, blog post, some other way to add value] I thought you'd enjoy, given your interest in [topic]."

- **Set calendar reminders to check in within two weeks if you haven't heard back (via phone, email, or both).**
- **Check in periodically with your top 10 contacts.** Check in with all other contacts at least twice a year. You can automate this by using a service like AWeber or Mailchimp to draft check-in emails to your entire contact list, sending mail-merged emails through Microsoft Outlook two to four times per year, setting up Google Alerts for your top 10 contacts to see if they're being mentioned in the news and follow up accordingly, or routinely scanning your LinkedIn for promotions, career changes, and publications from your contacts as fodder for a quick "ping" of congratulations.

Exceptional networkers are masters at the decisive step in our process: artful follow-up. So many people run into each other at conferences or meetings, but they never take the time to send a follow-up email or to schedule a quick check-in a few weeks later. Even the most well-meaning allies won't remember you in three weeks if you don't do the follow-up work needed to stay current in their minds.

Upgrading Your Inner Circle

As you begin moving forward toward your dream, chances are you are going to start feeling a little bit of discomfort when hanging with people who aren't moving forward as quickly as you are. The painful truth is that we often wind up as an average of our six closest friends. We tend to absorb some of each other's habits, interests, and even attitudes about life. Depending on who your six closest contacts are, this truth either thrills you or chills you to the core. Chances are, the thought of becoming an amalgam of your six closest friends today is less than thrilling. So, how do you shift your friendships to make room for people who will push you toward your dream?

It's a valid question, and a challenging one, particularly because it involves being honest with ourselves about the people we love most in the world. Here's the good news: I don't believe in an all-or-nothing approach to upgrading your circle. Instead, I believe the most sustainable way to get more out of (and to give more to) your relationships is to grow your network to include new, ambitious friends AND expect more out of the relationships you already have.

Find New Friends by Altering Your Behavior

One of the most important ways to make new friends is to do things that the kind of friends you want would be doing. If you want friends interested in entrepreneurship, spend less time at a bar and more time taking classes or attending meetups on entrepreneurship. If you want friends who are more serious about their craft as musicians, go to where the good musicians play and practice. Be more of the person you want to attract, and the right people will start showing up.

Redefine Relationships with Old Friends and Family Members

Let's be honest, cutting off all friends and family members who don't agree with your dream (or aren't as ambitious themselves) is unrealistic, foolish, and cruel. While there are some people you are going to have to drop from your life, most of the important people who are in your life need to stay there.

With that said, it is your responsibility to ensure these relationships don't stall you on the path to your dreams. To do this, you'll need to redefine what activities, conversations, and fellowship time is appropriate to keep these relationships thriving without sacrificing your dreams.

- **Your time.** One lever you can pull to redefine your relationships is being more disciplined about the time you spend with the people you love. Rather than spending four hours a week of low-quality, low-engagement time (watching TV, hanging out, clubbing, etc.), you can spend an hour or two every month in high-value time (rich conversation, doing meaningful, engaging activities together). This frees up over a dozen hours of time for you each month, while making your relationship stronger.

- **Your conversation.** One of the most damaging pieces of a "sandbag" relationship is the unfruitful, attitude-altering conversations it enables. Instead of spending time joking, gossiping, or complaining about life, raise the bar of conversation in your relationships. One way you might do this is focusing on solutions, not just problems. Another might be redirecting gossipy conversations when they're happening. At first, shifting conversations or even directly discussing why you don't want to talk about *x or y* will be uncomfortable, but it is an activity that will yield huge results in your friendship.

- **Your physiology.** Research indicates that one of the most powerful things friends can do together is complete varied, challenging physical activities. Whether that's going for a hike together, running a half-marathon, or simply playing basketball or taking a dance class, using your time together to increase your physical energy level and stamina lets you support each other and yourselves in a powerful way.

Do your best to think objectively about your areas of strength, hard skills, and expertise. What are they?

_____

_____

_____

_____

_____

In a nutshell, what do you do better than anyone else?

_____

_____

_____

_____

_____

How could you share this skill with the professional contacts you meet in pursuit of your dream?

_____

_____

_____

_____

_____

What are one or two content-specific areas that you read or study often (leadership, marketing, sales, etc.)?

_____

_____

_____

_____

_____

How could you leverage your insider knowledge of these areas to help the professional contacts you meet?

_____

_____

_____

_____

_____

How would you rate your networking abilities to date? How big is your network of allies?

_____

_____

_____

_____

_____

What is your current networking process? How can you tweak that process to yield even better results for you?

_____

_____

_____

_____

_____

What is one takeaway from this networking crash course that you will build into your networking system immediately?

_____

_____

_____

_____

_____

_____

_____

Which of the steps in the crash course is the hardest for you? Why? What will you do to upgrade your skills in this area?

_____

_____

_____

_____

_____

_____

_____

_____

Think about your inner circle. Are there people in your circle who are not adding value to you whom you need to cut off? If so, what's your plan to make that happen?

_____

_____

_____

_____

_____

_____

_____

Are there relationships in your circle that need to be redefined? What's your plan for redefining these relationships, while pursuing your dream?

_____

_____

_____

_____

_____

_____

_____

Do you need to find new friends who are more aligned to where you are going? What is your plan to alter your habits and behaviors to locate these friends?

_____

_____

_____

_____

_____

What relationships will you cultivate now to help you achieve your dream?

_____

_____

_____

_____

_____

Free Training Video:

Before you proceed visit the link below.
www.LiveYourDreamsOutLoud.com/book-Connecting

Competence

"Whenever you are asked if you can do a job,
tell 'em, 'Certainly I can!' Then get busy
and find out how to do it."

Theodore Roosevelt

Chapter 4:

Competence and Becoming World-Class

- How to examine competency
- The different levels of competence and incompetence
- How to execute intentional practice
- Soft skills vs hard skills
- Becoming a student of your craft

Often, the only tempo people try to operate at is instant, and we find ourselves wanting and expecting everything at the snap of our fingers. I refer to this as "the microwave society."

One of my greatest struggles with competence has been how long it takes to be really good at something. In fact, choosing competence often means choosing to move slower and more strategically than everyone else. Moving slowly, investing in what's under the surface before I put myself out there, and choosing the unbeaten path doesn't come easily to me.

To say that I have tried to rush my dream journey is an understatement. When I initially set out on my dream journey, I decided I wanted to accomplish a lot of things in a short amount of time. I sought out all the tips and tricks to shortcut my learning curve. On several occasions, I considered slow processes and incremental improvement as inefficient and unsatisfactory. What I've learned through this process is that **competency takes time**. You either pay upfront in preparation, building credibility, planning and strategizing, or you pay later in weak results and setbacks you aren't prepared to handle.

Even though I thought I wanted to fast-track my path to success, and even though I once shunned what I saw as small and measured steps on the way, I realized that I've actually been working on my dream for longer than anyone might know. It started well before that tragic moment years ago. I made the first conscious investment in my dream to be a speaker, media personality, and coach in 2008 when I enrolled in a $1,000 course by James Malinchak called "How to Become a Speaker." At the time, I'd already spent dozens of hours addressing thousands of students and had begun to see the impact of my work firsthand. What I was looking for was an accelerant to my success as a speaker, so I dug deep and purchased it, leaving me with a mere $100 to my name.

For me, investing in my own competence was the answer to shaving time from my learning curve and to improving rapidly in a few key areas. Counting the courses I purchased, the mentorship, and the seasons of unpaid internships I worked in order to garner experience, and the dozens of conferences and networking opportunities I've attended, I've easily invested a lot of money and thousands of hours working my dream. For most people, investing that kind of money and time into a dream might seem unconscionable. Good thing you and I aren't like most people. If you don't believe in yourself enough to put your time and money where your mouth is, why should anyone else?

Since I'm in the entertainment industry, I had industry-specific items to learn that could only be learned on the job. Every job has facets and intricacies you'll only learn from showing up and doing your job every day. For example, I've learned how the supervising producer manages the elements of production, how the executive producer/showrunner oversees the show as a whole, what questions the segment producer asks during the pre-interview with the talent, how to find props quickly, and how the talent booker/producer manages the relationships with the publicist, agents and manager while simultaneously building with talent.

By now, you get that I've been learning and cutting down on the hours in order to become more competent to live my dreams.

Examining competency

Whether your dream is to launch a business, get a law degree, or even be a world-class athlete, it will require you to be better than average. Depending on the boldness of your dream, it may even require you to be exceptional—in the top 10% of your peers. If you're serious, then it's time to sharpen your skills to be truly excellent at the competencies needed to achieve your dream.

Competence is expensive, and not just from a financial standpoint. I know that money may be what's holding you back; in fact, I understand that so well that I've dedicated an entire chapter to it and outlined a plan for cash flow. But whether you have a bit of dough or whether you're broke as can be, developing competence requires you to invest time, energy, and sometimes money into yourself. It requires you to engage in experiences that will differentiate you from your competition. It means you will have to let go of some of the diversions and entertainment that your friends and family members participate in. It may mean staying up later or getting up earlier.

It takes a plan to be competent at your dream; it won't just happen. In fact, it'd be fair to say that I've sometimes struggled with a microwave mentality. As dreamers, we want to see results fast. But the competence journey is more about strategy than it is about speed.

What I had to learn is that competence gives us an edge as we compete with others for the same dream.

According to the Oxford English Dictionary, the word competent means "the ability to do something successfully or efficiently." Merriam Webster's Dictionary defines it as "having requisite or adequate ability or qualities...legally qualified..." In everyday language, when we say someone is competent, we usually mean they are skilled enough to do the job. In the case of your dreams, your level of competence will directly impact your confidence and your success in executing your vision.

The reputed psychologist Dr. Maslow proposed a four-tier model of competence for any field. I've frequently used this model to assess where my mentees are in relation to their purpose.

Regardless of where we start on the journey to our dream, the goal is the same: getting to a place where we are consciously

LEVELS OF INCOMPETENCE	LEVELS OF COMPETENCE
Level One: Unconscious Incompetence – You are so novice at a field or at an endeavor that you don't realize how incompetent you are. You don't know how to improve, or even that you need to improve.	**Level One:** Unconscious Competence – You are successful at the endeavor you are undertaking, but you aren't sure why. Success is haphazard and not replicable, because you don't know what you are doing that's making you successful.
Level Two: Conscious Incompetence – You are learning more about the field or endeavor you're planning to undertake and realize the areas where you need to develop. You are not competent yet, but you are on your way to being competent.	**Level Two:** Conscious Competence – You have learned about the field or endeavor enough that you know exactly what you are doing to make yourself successful. Replicating success is easy because you know what you are doing to make yourself successful.

competent of the steps it takes to be successful and actively taking those steps.

Executing intentional practice

What does it take to be truly competent at anything? Four years of expensive courses to get a degree? Maybe, but not usually. The truth is, preparation is the heart and soul of competence. Appropriate, specific practice for the endeavor you're about to undertake is the best thing you can do to ensure your success.

Geoff Colvin, researcher, and author of Talent Is Over-rated, states that the difference between success and failure in any endeavor is intentional practice. Deliberate practice is the specific practice of the exact skills needed for mastery, with an eye for correcting and improving your performance.

In the book, Colvin lays out how what we typically attri-bute to "talent" is actually roughly 10,000 hours of intentional, specific practice in an endeavor. From Bill Gates to the Beat-les, and even to Mozart, the people we typically credit with exceptional genius had exceptional circumstances in their lives that allowed them to practice their craft for over 10,000 hours before becoming known as "world-class."

1. List out the specific skills that people successful at your dream have to master..

2. Choose one specific skill to focus on first and break that skill down to its component parts.

3. Practice the steps needed to do that one component really, really well until you are **perfect or nearly perfect**

COMPETENCE

takes

TIME

LIVE YOUR DREAMS OUT LOUD

at that component.

4. Move on to the next component(s) until you've mastered all aspects of that skill.

But Isn't It Useful to Be a Jack-of-All-Trades?

You might have heard that being well-versed in several domains makes you an asset, particularly if you have ever worked in the nonprofit and corporate sectors. In some industries, knowing how to do a few unique things rather than focus on just one makes you an especially useful middle-tier *worker*. The challenge—whether your dream is to play a sport, start a company, or anything else where the competition is fierce—is that being a jack-of-all-trades but a master of none *will handicap you*. That's because what people want in the highest tiers of influence (politically, in business, in entertainment, you name it) are world-class *masters,* not just useful workers. The ones at the top focus on one thing and learn it to mastery.

Let's be honest: do you really believe that being a jack-of-all-trades is the right path to take to your dreams? Of course not. Subconsciously, we choose this path because it feels much safer to throw things at the wall to see what sticks than it does to choose one thing and stick with it. None of us may acknowledge that as a dominant belief in our lives, but think about how we behave.

When we struggle to focus on one dream or one path to

that dream at a time, what we're saying is we believe that our future is in our busy-ness, not in our strategic activity. The truth is, specialization is what you need when it comes to succeeding at your dreams. We all know that. The real issue is, specialization takes courage. It requires us to close off options.

That's what we're afraid of.

Decide to face your fear and move forward. That's the only way to carry out your dreams at the scale you're dreaming them.

Soft Skills vs. Hard Skills

Have you ever met someone who was excellent at carrying out the technical aspects of their work but they were terrible with people? You can almost bet that, unless something changed, they were going to be stifled (or jailed) on the path to achieving their dreams with a reputation for being cut-throat in pursuit of their goals. Maybe they were just creepy, and no one wanted to be around them or do business with them because they had no tact or social skills. A person with limited interpersonal skills, no matter how technically competent, is going to cut off or limit their success in the marketplace.

On the other hand, have you ever met someone who was incredibly nice but totally incompetent? If you purchased anything from them (you probably didn't), it was out of guilt or pity, not because they offered something of value. This individual will have a tough time scaling their success once their family, friends, and other immediate supporters have already purchased from them. Since they don't have any real "hard skills," it's difficult for them to move forward with their dream.

I wish I could tell you that having a big dream, being kind, and being deeply passionate about your success will guarantee that your dream will come true. Unfortunately, the opposite is true. Even if you are the nicest person in the world, and even if you are determined to be successful, you will go nowhere without attending to competence. At the same time, if you struggle with interacting with people, you can't brush that under the rug by believing your technical skill will cover that weakness. No matter what business you are in, for the near future, you will be buying from and selling to people.

As a dreamer, you must master both your hard skills (technical skills, the "what" of your dream) and soft skills (your ability to cultivate supporters and influence people). Both will contribute powerfully to your success.

Becoming a Student of Your Craft

For most of us, competence and study go hand in hand. Study your craft and learn what key thinkers in your field are saying and doing. If you're a singer, becoming a student of your craft might look like taking voice lessons with a world-class coach. If your dream is to become a stellar lawyer for a top-tier law firm, you will need to study and take courses to nail the LSAT exam—a core component of any law school application. If your dream is to start a marketing firm, then you need to study the components of online and offline marketing, either at the graduate school level or via the highest-ranked books in the field.

Every dream is different, so every path is different, but the bottom line is that you need to determine what information you need to know that you don't know already and to develop a plan for acquiring and acting on that information.

Although it's tempting to do so, don't rush the process to become competent. Lay out a plan to become competent in the area your dream entails and stick to it.

Becoming competent takes time, investment, and physical and mental effort. How much time, what kind of financial investment, and the intensity of physical and mental effort you contribute will directly impact how successful you will be.

Pre-Work: What Competency Does Your Dream Require?

What skills, competencies, certifications, or other prerequisites does this dream require?

_____

_____

_____

_____

_____

_____

Think about your dream. Where would you place yourself in the competence journey? Why?

_____

_____

_____

_____

_____

What are the specific skills people who are going to be world-class at your dream must master?

_____

_____

_____

_____

On a scale of 1-10, where are you with each of those skills?

_____

_____

_____

_____

_____

Which of these skills is the most important to being successful at your dream?

_____

_____

_____

_____

_____

What will you need to do to master this skill?

_____

_____

_____

_____

Think about the dream you have chosen to pursue. What does being a student of that dream look like? What courses might you have to take? What books will you have to read? Be specific.

_____

_____

_____

_____

What are the areas you will learn more about and practice in, in the next 12 months, to improve your competence? How much time will you devote to each of these areas each month in order to grow your competence? What resources will you purchase (or which practice activities will you participate in) to develop yourself in these areas?

AREA OF COMPETENCE	TIME NEEDED (PER WEEK)	MY PLAN FOR DEVELOPING IN THIS AREA

Dream Spotlight: Tim Ferriss and "Selective" Competence

New York Times best-selling author Tim Ferriss is an interesting example of "selective" competence. Tim isn't a master at traditional business or public speaking (although he is a master of loopholes, acceleration strategies, and winning as efficiently as possible). It didn't take Tim twenty years (or even five years) to build a profitable business. Once he zeroed in on the key levels to success in his industry (first the diet and drug industry, then information marketing), he was able to exponentially increase his progress in just a year.

Since then, he's published three significant best sellers: *The Four-Hour Work Week*; *The Four-Hour Body*; and *The Four-Hour Chef* in just 5 years. He's won elite awards in Chinese San Shou and competed in Argentine Tango Competitions—all with focused, short-term, intense competency-building activities. He advises his followers that they can become functionally fluent in any language in three months or less. In short, he believes that competence is key, but he's able to focus on the key aspects needed for 80% competence, then he drills those into his brain as quickly and as efficiently as possible.

If nothing else, Tim proves that competence doesn't need to take a lifetime if you focus on the key levels of your dream and learn them deeply and well. He also proves that you can't fake it. Even if you try to take shortcuts, there are core skills you will need to learn in order to be successful.

***Free Training Video*:**
Before you proceed visit the link below.
www.LiveYourDreamsOutLoud.com/book-Competence

Conditioning

There is no way to be truly great in this world.
We are all impaled on the crook of conditioning.

James Dean

Chapter 5:

Conditioning Yourself to Chase Your Dream

In this chapter, you'll discover:
- Why conditioning yourself mentally and physically is so important to the LYDOL process
- How to condition yourself to live your dreams out loud
- Ways to combat any previous conditioning that's blocking your pathway to the future

Conditioning is a system of training that prepares you for a significant challenge. It's hard to activate the dream if there are mental blocks in the way that stem from how you've been conditioned. It doesn't matter who you are; we all come from home environments inflicted with the thoughts and perspectives of others. The environment in which you were raised plays a large part on your mental conditioning. This is not a knock at your upbringing or your hometown, but good or bad, your environment conditioned you to think, act, and believe a certain way.

I need to say that I believe I have one of the best families in the world, but growing up in Skipperville conditioned me to be a *worker*. It seemed like the best path you could take towards finding "the job" was to go to college. As a boy, I made a decision that nothing in the world was going to keep me from college. Every time I sold pencils with the emblems of college teams to my classmates, every time I hustled for a job cutting hair or doing odd chores, I had one dream in mind: going to college. I'd done everything I knew to prepare myself mentally, physically, and emotionally to get a scholarship to be there.

As a smart, talented, and driven high school athlete, I thought getting a college scholarship to a Division 1 school would be pretty much guaranteed. I was 6'2" and a seasoned guard/forward, with experience playing against much taller, bigger players. I had a great relationship with my coaches and teachers and knew I'd get glowing recommendations. I knew that I wouldn't get into all my top choices, but I figured if I cast my net wide enough, I'd get at least one yes. When I was denied a scholarship from every D-1 school I applied to in the middle of my senior year, the disappointment hit me like a punch to the chest.

That's when my find-a-way inner hustler kicked in. It's hard to overstate how much my struggles as a kid prepared me for the disappointments of my senior year. As a young entrepreneur, I had to bounce back from rejection and lost sales dozens of times. My ability to bounce back, undaunted, from these failures and to keep fighting for a yes was vital to securing a college scholarship and more importantly, a college degree.

Now that I had hit a little turbulence, I knew it was game time. Either I would step up and find a way, or I would forfeit my college dream forever.

I knew I didn't win a scholarship for a simple reason: I was too short to play a college forward. The problem was, that was the only position I'd played in high school. There were other positions my height and physicality would be a great match for, but I couldn't play them at the college level. So, I devised a plan to work out and practice three times a day, then pitch schools on doing an in-person tryout for their teams. My mom drove me to tryout after tryout, and I received no after no, until we got a yes from Enterprise State Junior College.

Most in my family believe in that "good job" notion and aren't risk takers, and I was conditioned to partake in that mentality, too. I was supposed to go get that respectable job after college. That's why I had been working hard towards the dream of college all those years! I'd transferred to the University of Alabama, and I was in my junior year when I learned that Philip Morris USA (a company that recruited heavily from Alabama's business school) loved to recruit candidates who worked at Enterprise Rent-a-Car. At that time, I was looking for the job opportunity that paid the most, with the most benefits.

I had a mutual friend who worked there full-time and if given the opportunity, I could sell myself and get the job. I cold-called Enterprise and went in to speak with the manager whose name was Joe Kraus. I explained to Joe that I was looking for an internship. It didn't matter if it was a paying gig or not. I was looking for an opportunity because I was looking to have all my ducks in a row for Philip Morris my senior year when they came back to recruit during the fall/spring of my senior year.

While at Enterprise, I bumped into another acquaintance who was working at Enterprise. Mario Bailey and I were both Greek, and although not members of the same fraternity, we knew of each other. Because of his blessings, he confirmed with the GM that it would be a good reason to bring me on board, and he put in a good word for me. Mario and I are still great friends to this day. Thank you, Mario (DAB). I was given the internship at Enterprise, and it was a *paid* internship. I learned a lot about customer service and selling while at Enterprise and made some lifelong relationships.

During my senior year, Philip Morris came back to recruit and were only looking to hire two individuals from the business school out of thousands of applicants. I had taken the necessary steps and established myself to be on their radar by engaging and adding value to the recruiter years before. Only two of us got the job: me and Clayton Shockley. I was assigned to Huntsville, Alabama where I would be managing a territory of 170-plus chain and independent stores. The territory was doing upwards of $27 million dollars in revenue, and I had been hired on the fast track, which meant they wanted to give me a large amount of responsibility and develop me to be a leader within the company.

My starting salary was $53,500 and came with a company car and other great benefits, including a chance to earn a bonus. I'd never seen that much money and thought it would be a cool job and not too strenuous. I didn't see myself being in the job forever, but I knew that I needed to do something, and I didn't want to stay in school anymore. I had somehow convinced and tricked myself that I was going to thrive in this corporate space.

While I was in this position, all my friends were going to grad/law school or pursuing pharmaceutical and engineering jobs. They seemed content doing these things whether they were conditioned to it or whether these paths were their true dreams. When I reflect on this time period, I can now see

CONDITIONING

is a

SYSTEM OF TRAINING THAT PREPARES YOU

for a **SIGNIFICANT CHALLENGE.**

that I was a follower, and I really didn't have a clue what I wanted to do.

If you are going to be on the path of living your dreams, it's important to break the conditioning of what you've been taught and what mentality is holding you back.

Three components to conditioning

Today, whenever preparing for a new challenge, I am reminded by the mental and physical conditioning that shaped me as a young one. This ability to keep moving forward, despite setbacks has served me well as a motivational speaker, coach, consultant, and entrepreneur. I realized that are three important aspects to develop in order to change our conditions:

- Emotional/spiritual conditioning
- Mental conditioning
- Physical conditioning

Developing Emotional Resilience

How good are you at managing your emotions? Do crises send you over the edge? Do you freeze in tough situations?

Pursuing your dreams is a wild ride full of exciting victories and crushing setbacks. Family members and dear friends are sometimes extremely supportive; other times, they're your dream's worst nightmare.

Most dreamers give up along the way, simply due to emotional exhaustion. That's why cultivating emotional toughness—the ability to keep your emotions at a functional level, no matter what—is a needed skill.

My first three months at Philip Morris were ok. I was making decent money, and I had the autonomy to come and go as I pleased. The problem was that as a black man assigned to this particular territory, I wasn't welcomed by some of the owners in the backwoods stores. This made me reluctant to continue carrying on with my job responsibilities. One day it dawned on me that I wasn't where I was supposed to be in my life. While walking to my car outside of a store, a car went by and a white man yelled, *"You fucking nigger, go back to where you came from."* I immediately requested a transfer out of that territory because I felt my life had been threatened. After reporting that incident, nothing was done about it immediately.

I started to hate my job and would lay in bed not wanting to go in at all. I developed such an elevated level of stress that I made frequent trips to the hospital for examinations. It was there that I tapped into my faith, made a stance and asked God to take me through whatever he wanted in order for my purpose to be revealed.

Developing a sense of spiritual awareness is integral to your emotional conditioning.I had been raised in the heart of the Bible belt, and I grew up in an AME (African Methodist Episcopal) church. My great-grandmother, who played a key role in my upbringing, saw herself as the queen of the church since she was a devout believer, a church leader, and an encourager. I'm sharing this because I came from an environment heavily rooted in Christianity, and that foundation is still part of my life today. Sure, my spiritual life has stretched beyond my AME roots, but the roots haven't disintegrated.

Even if you weren't brought up to be religious or if you are non-spiritual from a society standpoint, it's important that you believe in the spirit of yourself and that you stand for something. When it comes to spiritual conditioning, I fundamentally believe we all have our different ways of obtaining spiritual conditioning. My challenge to anyone who is reading this is to not allow your upbringing and what you were taught as it relates to faith to be your only reference. Sometimes, we are conditioned spiritually through some sort of life experience. I challenge those to step out of their comfort zone and connect with the things that are constant and will remain, such as water, air, nature, and stillness. Being still can allow you to open up in ways and experience a deeper connection with self and with the universe.

Here are a few steps you can follow to toughen-up your emotions and condition yourself spiritually:

1. **Know Yourself:** Know what situations tend to push you over the edge. Know how your body responds when you are emotionally compromised. For example, when you're angry, do you ball your fists and grit your teeth? Do you withdraw and retreat? By knowing your triggers and what you do, you can develop a plan B and flip the "calm" switch when you feel triggered.

2. **Prepare for All Options:** For most people, one of the biggest triggers of being emotionally compromised is having an unforeseen disappointment or stressful

outcome. By determining what you will do if a situation doesn't go as you planned, you are more likely to follow the best course of action.

3. **Keep the Pillars of Your Life Stable:** There are only a few things in life that really matter: our health, our family, and having our basic necessities met. Being able to keep those things stable and in working order makes it easier to adapt to disappointments in other areas of life. If at all possible, keep the most basic areas of your life as drama-free as possible.

Mental Toughness

While emotional resilience has to do with keeping your inner world as peaceful and as stable as possible, mental toughness helps you triumph when your inner world is going crazy.

For me, the most important conditioning in my life happened off the field as I have cultivated the mental toughness to keep pursuing my dreams, even when faced with significant challenges.

Mental toughness is the ability to keep your mind and body focused on your goal, despite significant challenges to its success. The more significant a goal is to you personally or professionally, the more stress you may feel as you pursue it. Mental toughness is the strength to push through that stress in order to be successful.

Like most other "muscles," the mental toughness muscle increases in strength as you challenge it. That's why many people who succeed professionally and in other areas embrace challenge, such as choosing to run long races or to participate in other endurance challenges

Here are a few steps you can follow to toughen-up your emotions and to condition yourself mentally:

1. **Be honest to yourself**
2. **Find your inner peace**
3. **Get comfortable being uncomfortable**

Cultivating Physical Toughness

Have you noticed that some of the most successful and wealthy executives, Wall Street wizards and musicians are serious about physical activity? Have you also noticed that low-income individuals tend to be much less physically active? One of the reasons this trend prevails is that physical fitness is a "trigger" habit, which is a habit that triggers other habits.

Another reason to cultivate physical strength, health, and toughness is that pursuing any worthwhile dream demands a lot from you. Working your day job and your night grind is exhausting. Having your body in less-than-optimal shape will curtail what you can do.

Have you ever met the perpetually sick entrepreneur? Due to a lack of sleep, abundance of stress, and no time to take care of themselves physically, they battle a cough, headache, or even body pain that just doesn't go away.

I've met them. In fact, I've been them.

Learning to take care of myself includes resting when I

need to, eating better, and protecting the time to work out regularly. This has been critical to sustaining my momentum over time.

Additionally, physical activity helps a lot with stress management. If, like me, you struggle to make good decisions in stressful situations, exercise can give you the much-needed space and perspective to see situations clearly.

People who can force themselves to work out, even when they don't want to, can often "trigger" other positive habits, like balancing a checkbook or keeping their apartment clean. For example, even though I was redshirted my entire freshmen year, as I practiced and improved my skills, I eventually played well and often for our team. More importantly, I learned to keep fighting for my dream.

Conversely, people who struggle with their eating and exercise often struggle in other areas as well. They're not chasing their dreams.

At its core, physical toughness has three facets:

1. **Self-Management:** Being able to motivate yourself to take a needed action, even when you are mentally or physically exhausted. Self-management helps you stick to a fitness regimen, even when tired or busy.

2. **Mastery:** Sticking with a routine until you are able to master it, no matter how long it takes. Mastery provokes you to continue a workout routine or a new skill until you succeed.

3. **Testing Limits:** Forcing yourself to do more than what was previously possible. Testing your limits helps you disprove fear, and achieve outlandish goals.

Each of these facets does more than just improve your health; they also provide transferable skill sets and mindsets that you can implement in other areas.

Dreamer Spotlight: Olympians and Conditioning

While it's easy to think that Olympic athletes are just born talented, history tells us a different story: elite athletes have participated in at least 10,000 hours of grueling practice before winning their fame. Typical studies about the habits of world-class athletes reveal that the average elite athlete (Olympian, pro-NBA player, etc.) spent 23 hours per week intentionally practicing their skill, for at least 8 years, before becoming world-class (www.strengthplanet.com).These practices are rigorous and thoughtful, draining, and focused.

Michael Phelps is the poster boy for intentional practice. He doesn't do 100 exercises in the gym or in the pool. Instead, he focuses his effort on the ones that have the greatest effect on his swimming: exercises that boost his upper body strength so that his strokes can have the greatest impact. Phelps also well-exceeds the average for elite athletes: he trains for approximately 36 hours and swims roughly 50 miles each week. As a result of his intentional, focused practice, he has won over 71 world medals in the Olympic, Pan-Pacific Championships, and World Championships, holds several world records in swimming and has won multiple awards. He's done this by being a remarkable swimmer, but also by being an even better student and practitioner of his craft.

If we step out of the pool and into the gym, we can see similar excellence in gymnast Gabrielle Douglas. In her case, conditioning meant beginning gymnastics classes as young as two years old. It meant spending much of her childhood at practices, competitions, or on the road traveling. It also meant enduring a painful wrist fracture, and having to heal, practice, and make up for a year of lost time. All the while, she endured racial slurs and persecution. Still, Douglas took the world by storm by winning the gold all-around medal and contributing to her team's all-around gold win at the 2012 Olympics. We started seeing her name everywhere: Corn Flakes boxes, Nintendo commercials, onstage at the MTV Video Music Awards. Imagine the mental toughness it takes to spend more than twelve hours a week practicing your craft for the first fifteen years of your life. This is the kind of dedication it takes to perform in front of the entire world and shine.

Whether your dream is to be a world-class singer, a top-ranked lawyer or surgeon, or a clergyman, the process is the same: anticipating the challenges you will face on the way to your dream, and cultivating the physical, emotional, and mental toughness to overcome those challenges.

Would you consider yourself a physically strong person?
Why or why not?

_____

_____

_____

_____

_____

What can you do to take better care of yourself physically,
as you pursue your dreams?

_____

_____

_____

_____

_____

Would you consider yourself emotionally strong and
resilient? Why?

_____

_____

_____

_____

_____

What are the triggers that set you off emotionally? What happens when you are emotionally compromised? What types of mistakes do you tend to make?

_____

_____

_____

_____

_____

What steps can you take today to simplify the pillars of your life, so you'll have a deep reserve of emotional stability?

_____

_____

_____

_____

What are some areas where your mental toughness has allowed you to persevere, in spite of challenges?

_____

_____

_____

_____

What are some areas where you have not met the mark, due to a lack of mental toughness?

_____

_____

_____

_____

_____

What are some challenges you can take on, in order to increase your mental toughness?

_____

_____

_____

_____

_____

Free Training Video:

Before you proceed visit the link below.

www.LiveYourDreamsOutLoud.com/book-Conditioning

Cash Flow

"The sheriff is at the cash register, and if I don't get a hit soon, I don't know what I'll do."

—Nat King Cole

Cash Flow and Resourcing Your Dream

In this chapter, you'll discover:
* How to maintain a stream of income while pursuing your dream
* How to manage your finances during this phase
* Ways to fund your dreams into reality

The Cashflow Trap

You made it! You've decided what you want to do, you've conditioned yourself, you've determined how to become competent enough to do it, and you've committed to your goal and made the right connections. Now your dream will just happen, right? Not so fast.

The reason most dreamers never accomplish their plan has a lot to do with the steps we've already covered, but it also has to do with the last step in your dream journey: developing a plan to resource your dream financially. For most dreamers, budgeting and accumulating cash to sustain their dream is the part of their dream they dodge like the plague.

I'll be honest: this step has always been a struggle for me.

I'm not motivated by money; I never have been. I do things because they're important, whether they'll be financially profitable or not. What I've had to learn is that sustaining your dream takes cash. Without adequate cash flow, you'll eventually have to give up your dream in order to buy groceries and put a roof over your head.

That's why cash is not a "nice-to-have" where your dream is concerned—it's foundational. By prioritizing savings and profitability, you'll make your dream more sustainable over time and increase your chances of success.

Despite how much dreamers hate it, finding the cash to launch and sustain their dream is the defining factor between dreamers who launch (and fail) and those who succeed. Think about it: chances are, you personally have avoided the subject of stockpiling cash for your dream for any of the following reasons:

- The need to finance your dream intimidates you. Given your history with saving or your current expenses, you doubt your ability to successfully fund your dream.
- You associate finding cash to fund your dream with self-deprivation; you think you have lived a boring, cheap life to actively save for your dream.
- For ambitious people who enjoy moving as quickly as possible, saving for their dream feels too slow a route to accomplishing it. They'd rather launch now and worry about the money later.

How do you go from running a $350,000 a year business to sleeping on a friend's couch in just twelve months? How do you find yourself near bankrupt in a business that once brought in $15,000 in just a few days? How do you go from a well-paying job to having to scratch together a few hundred dollars to head to California for a chance at an unpaid internship? Simple: by not monitoring your cash flow.

As a dreamer, I've often found myself battling an interesting tension where money is concerned. On the one hand, growing up in a struggling household, I found myself worrying about money constantly. On the other hand, as a dreamer, I found myself avoiding hard conversations, with clients and with myself, about money. It's like a part of me was in denial about the fact that money was crucial to accomplishing my dreams.

The trick of mastering cash flow is about figuring out how much you need to live and then finding a source for that income that will sustain you while you build your dream. If that source of income is in a related area, or feeds your soul in some other way, that's even better. If it doesn't, take the job and hustle diligently in order to leave quickly. Most importantly, I've learned that there's nothing valiant or noble about struggling financially if you don't have to. It's not a rite of passage. It's better to bankroll your dream then to lose it due to poor planning. Embrace your need to master cash-flow and you'll be one step closer to living your dreams.

Personally, I have struggled with several of these challenges myself, so I know how real they are to us as dreamers. With that said, I can tell you unequivocally that some of the most painful experiences I and other dreamers have experienced on our journey to success could have been avoided with more attention to this topic.

Dreamers need a day job for the meantime

The revelation that I could do work I really enjoyed while planning for the business I would love was an important one for me. Previously, I had the flawed mindset that if I worked a job, I'd be stealing time and energy from my dream. In short, I saw a full-time job as selling myself and my dream short.

As a result, I struggled.

When I finished with Philip Morris, I asked God to take me through whatever He wanted in order for me to understand my purpose.

Well, He did.

A few months after someone called me a nigger, I was fired on a technicality that I wasn't aware of. During that time, my computer had begun to fail me, and I had to submit it in for a new one. When I got my computer back, all my calls and visits to the stores had to be manually entered. I entered that I had visited a store that was closed for whatever reason, and to the company, that was considered falsifying a call. I didn't know this at the time. I thought if the store was closed, you enter successful because I wasn't aware of another option. Regardless, it was my fault, but I felt as if this was their way of wanting to get rid of me.

Numerous leaders in the company called me and told me not to let this go and to pursue it on another level, but I was ready to be done with this and to begin to explore a different route. Ironically, prior to my termination, I was planning on going to Phoenix, Arizona to attend a party hosted by Fonzworth Bentley and Matt Leinart. My friend Kenny King was playing for the Arizona Cardinals at the time, and it was the weekend of my birthday. Kenny is a cousin of my best friend Corey who also played a part in me choosing the University of Alabama. I didn't know that I would be terminated the week of, but I wasn't letting that stop me. When I visited Phoenix, it felt right, and it was so liberal and different than I was used to. At the time, I didn't have any other means of cash flow, but I had close to $5K saved and decided to pack my bags and head west. As I mentioned, Kenny was playing in the NFL but had a few businesses at the time. I felt I could help add value to his window-tinting business that focused on residential, commercial, and automotive window tinting. This entrepreneurial venture was one that I accredit as the most important to my entrepreneurial journey. With long nights trying to figure out ways to generate revenue, acquire new customers and market and advertise our business buy driving down the freeway and getting off at every stop and nailing a sign at each stop light, I was getting a taste of the true entrepreneurial hustle.

After months of busting my ass day and night, we had grown and were on par to do roughly $350K that year in revenue. We were a small business with the capability of growing and expanding and becoming a force of reckoning. Myspace was big at the time and Facebook was just getting started. Online marketing wasn't as prevalent as it is today. A lot of our business was from a blinds company; anytime they sold blinds, they would sell window tint as a way of lowering a client's power bill.

They sold this to homes and businesses. Also, we had a contract with Lexus where we tinted their high-end vehicles.

After months of busting my ass and growing the business, Kenny decided he didn't want the business anymore and wanted to invest his time in other areas. Kenny had invested into the business and took ownership and control from the original founder who was now one of the primary installers. Since Kenny owned the business outright, he thought I would be good to run and own the business and decided to sell the business to me for $1 and gave me a $25K loan to invest into the business.

One of my biggest challenges in the business was finding ways for us to diversify our business and to generate revenue. Our contracts were set up in net 30s to make payments. We were relying heavily on those contracts, which generated a substantial amount of revenue when sold, and not so much our automotive clientele. This was also in 2007 when the economy was facing an economic downturn and the housing market sales were beginning to dry up. At that point in time, people stopped spending their money. I started seeing where I now had to pay my employees and not get paid myself. It was the right thing to do.

I didn't have a solid play in place to generate cash flow, and because of that, my business suffered, and I had to end up closing the doors. It's ridiculously hard to sustain and run a business if you don't have cash flow. It was my first Entrepreneur 101 experience, and I had to close the doors. Yes, it was a tough loss for sure, but I learned the lesson that if you don't find ways to be creative and implement cash flow in your business, then you don't have a business.

Five Poverty-Inducing Myths that Dreamers Believe

Since they're so detrimental to our success as dreamers, it's important that we clear the air where these ideas are concerned as quickly as possible.

Myth #1: I don't need cash for this dream

Tell any successful dreamer that you believe cash isn't needed to pursue your dream, and they will sorely disagree. The truth of the matter is, whether to fund the time, capital, training, or marketing/publicity needed to accomplish your dream, cash matters.

Time: At the very least, cash pays for the time needed to pursue your craft and move toward your dream. If you're struggling to make ends meet, the eight hours on a Saturday you could spend on your dream might be spent waiting tables or tutoring on the side. Ample savings gives you the ability to take an unpaid day of leave to pursue a speaking engagement or to meet with a mentor. Your time is the most valuable resource you have, but without cash, it will be brokered to one or more jobs to pay your bills.

Capital: Some dreams require physical resources to come to pass, whether that's a high-definition video camera, a new set of clippers, or even a piece of real estate. To get any of those things, you need money! To be clear, I believe many dreamers overestimate how much money they'll need to get started, but even if you bootstrap your own dream (we'll discuss that later), you're going to need some funds to purchase needed capital.

Training: If you want to be world-class at anything, you are probably going to need to enhance your skills through coursework, apprenticeship, coaching or reading. Training, especially effective, high-value training, is expensive. Without a cash engine to fund the learning needed to take your dream to the next level, you are likely to stagnate in your skill-set. While much practice will usually improve your ability, focused practice—like the kind you receive during expert training—is what truly separates exceptional athletes, performers, entrepreneurs, and other dreamers from mediocre ones.

Marketing & Publicity: Some dreams require a platform of loyal fans to come to fruition. An example of this might be publishing a nonfiction book, where your would-be publisher needs to know you have a following before they read your manuscript. Other examples might include selling CDs to secure funds for a tour or selling tickets to a live event. In any of these instances, securing marketing and publicity might require funds.

In all these instances, a lack of uncommitted, discretionary funds could severely hinder your dream from happening. Cash matters: *it isn't the most important thing, but that doesn't mean it isn't important.*

Myth #2: If I focus on making money, I will be a sell-out

As a dreamer, it's easy to see a focus on profitability as the enemy to being an "artist." Part of that has to do with a lie we're told in society that financially successful people are shallow and opportunistic, whereas starving artists are deep and principled.

SOMETIMES A JOB IS A HINDERANCE *to* **LIVING YOUR DREAM**

In practice, we know there are plenty of financially success-ful people who believe there is more to life than money and use their dreams and talents to make the world a more vibrant place. On the other hand, we also know there are plenty of "starving artists" who are irresponsible, selfish procrastinators who mooch off others and live below their potential. The truth is, whether you sell out your passion or not has less to do with your resource engine and more to do with your character.

Further, it's inaccurate to believe that monetizing some-thing diminishes its value as art. If we sold a Monet painting, or a Bach compilation, would that make those works of art less valuable? Does the fact that Michelangelo received financial compensation for the Sistine Chapel make it less beautiful or timeless? Of course not. Then why would we believe that by considering money as we build out our dream, we would be cheapening our art? I hope as you think this through, you discover this way of thinking just doesn't add up.

Myth #3: If I simply focus on executing my dream, the money will find me

So many aspiring dreamers believe this myth. I think it's by far the most prevalent and damaging to our community. The implicit idea in this myth is that seeking profitability is an unnecessary distraction. Instead, by focusing entirely on pro-ducing the best quality product you can (whether as a singer, a speaker, a student, etc.), the needed resources to fulfill your dream will just magically show up. This is especially a problem for spiritual people, because we tend to believe that our part is merely to produce the product, and Divine Providence will bring customers to pound down our door. *99.99% of the time, this is simply not the case.*

The Small Business Association alleges that 30% of new small businesses fail in their first year, and over half fail within five years. Many of those businesses fail because they are financially insolvent: they are unable to make enough money to stay afloat. I wish I could tell you that the reason they were financially failing had to do with a poor product. In some cases, this is certainly true, but it's not true for most of them. For many of these businesses, the problem is actually much more terrifying: an excellent product, a committed CEO, and a poor plan to achieve cash.

Someone might say, "Yes, that makes sense for business people, but my dream is different!" Is it, really? Even if your dream is to start a nonprofit that feeds orphans, simply doing good work won't pay your electricity bill. The IRS reports that 30,000-60,000 nonprofit organizations disappear from the IRS docket each year. Most of these vanish because they are financially failing. Just as in the case of the business, these organizations may offer a great service and address a real issue, but unless they can raise needed funds, they will not survive.

Even as an artist or musician, or even a pro-athlete, finding the right opportunities and handling the money aspects of your dream are pivotal. Why else would so many pro-athletes and all-star musicians, many of whom bring home millions of dollars in salary each year, be experiencing foreclosures and other money woes?

The bottom line is your talents don't necessarily equal business success. Without focusing in on securing the resources needed to be successful, you won't be.

Myth #4: A lack of money won't interfere with my dream

Most people who start a business, open a nonprofit, or try to make it as an artist, athlete, or other performer give up when they don't meet success. In fact, most people give up quickly—within the first few years—if they merely break even. As humans, we need affirmation that what we're doing is working. In fact, that's why most diets fail: because people aren't seeing the effects of their work as quickly or as consistently as they'd like.

It's true that you might be the .005% of the population who can persevere, for years, through a difficult challenge with little reinforcement or assurance of success. Chances are, you aren't, so why risk it?

Even if you are the kind of person who digs their heels in and won't give up, being profitable as you pursue your dream probably won't hurt you. While there is some validity of the hustle and innovation we see in people who have to bootstrap their own dreams and make it with limited resources, that doesn't mean a well-resourced person can't be equally creative. In fact, you could still force yourself to do more with less but have the money in stockpiles in case "less" doesn't work out the way you thought it would.

Finally, our society loves to cling to fantastic rags-to-riches stories as the dominant path that great people used to get to where they are. The truth is, many of the people we most respect were never "living out of a car" broke. They made wise choices and used resources well to create the empires we know today.

Creating the cash-flow plan

Simply by determining your cash plan intentionally, you'll be steps ahead of your peers who struggle financially for the first year or two in their business. More importantly, you will ensure your business will succeed in spite of any financial challenges you face.

Building an Out loud Fund to Resource Your Dream

The first step to building up reserves in order to resource you dream is to create an "Out loud Fund." This savings account has one purpose: to tuck away funds you can use to buy capital, training, or other services related to your dream. If you decide to eventually quit your job, this fund can also buy the time and effort it will take to get your dream off the ground.

When you're opening your account, you will want to make sure you do the following:

- Do not link the Out loud Fund to your checking account. You want to make it as hard as possible to transfer money from your Out loud Fund to your checking account.
- Create a custom name for the account that relates to your dream (e.g. The MBA Fund if your dream is to go back to college). This will make it harder to liquidate the account to pay for a day-to-day need. More importantly, every time you sign into your bank, you'll be reminded of the progress you are making on the road to your dream.

- Set up auto-deposits to ensure you are systematically growing this account over time. Even if your deposits are small, by consistently depositing into this account, you will be disciplining yourself to save toward your dream.

Once you set up your Out loud Fund, the next step is to figure out your savings strategy and how much money you'll need to use this account to accomplish your dream.

Determine Your Savings Strategy

It would be unrealistic to expect a one-size-fits-all savings strategy would be helpful to you on the path to funding your dream. Your savings strategy needs to match you: it needs to reflect where you are in life, what other commitments you already have, and what needs you have in relation to your dream.

For example, if you are a single, well-paid banker with no debt, and your dream is to move to the Bahamas and work remotely, you'll have vastly different savings goals than someone with three children who dreams of opening a hotel.

Further, your dream (and its potential to generate income) also informs your savings goals. If your dream is to increase your existing freelance business so you can quit your job, you may need less money to get started than if you dream of opening a string of orphanages in the developing world. If your dream is revenue-generating, then your savings strategy is short-term: what money do you need to accumulate to begin generating money? If your dream is not revenue-generating, you'll need to find a way to monetize it or to make enough money elsewhere to fund it for the long-haul.

Figuring Out How Much You Need

In order to focus your efforts, you're going to have to calculate "your number": the amount of savings needed to significantly launch your dream.

How much you need is relative to what your dream is, what investments **are needed** to make it happen, and whether or not your dream itself makes money once launched.

An important distinction is whether or not you are going to need to leave your full-time job in order to launch your dream. If you are, be sure to factor in the costs of your living expenses for at least the first three months of your launch.

––––––––––

How are you affected by financial risk? Do you panic when finances are a little tight? Do you become less motivated when there isn't financial pressure?

_____

_____

_____

_____

_____

_____

_____

_____

What financial commitments do you have? Debt? College tuition? Your parents? Considering these costs, how much can you afford to save each month?

_____

_____

_____

_____

_____

_____

_____

How much will your dream cost to execute? How much funds will actually need to be from you? Are there small business loans or other sources you can use to supplement your savings?

_____

_____

_____

_____

_____

_____

In light of these questions, will your savings strategy be aggressive or conservative? Will your current level of income allow you to save as you need to kickstart your dream?

_____

_____

_____

_____

_____

_____

_____

_____

Calculate the amount, per month, it will cost to launch and sustain your dream. Include the equipment, training, and other expenses but do not include nice-to-haves. Stick to the most basic costs. DO NOT INCLUDE LIVING EXPENSES.

_____

_____

_____

_____

_____

_____

_____

If your dream requires you to quit your job, determine the amount of money per month that is needed just to cover your basic living expenses. Be specific. Itemize your most needed expenses and tally the total. Multiply this number by three for three months of living expenses.

_____

_____

_____

_____

_____

_____

_____

_____

Add both numbers. This is the total amount needed to live your dream out loud for the first three months. What's your number?

_____

_____

_____

Knowing this number gives you a huge advantage over most dreamers. You now know exactly what your savings goal needs to be in order to launch your dream!

Proven Strategies to Stock Your Out loud Fund

Now that you've established exactly how much cash is needed to launch your dream, how do you get it?

The Staple of Your Out loud Fund: Your Full-time Income

The primary source for your Out loud Fund will be savings from your full-time salary and other income. By saving a consistent amount from each paycheck, over time, you will build a sizable fund for your dream.

To use this strategy:

1. Lower your monthly expenses by trimming unnecessary luxuries like eating out, extra benefits on your cell phone, and even cable television.
2. Use the extra cash you create to fund a savings account for your dream.

The Out loud Fund Accelerator: Your Side Hustle

In addition to saving your day-to-day income, another strategy is to start a side job or freelancing service in order to save additional funds. This acceleration strategy is an addition to the savings you earn from your day-to-day labor.

To use this strategy:

1. Brainstorm potential sources of on-the-side income (freelancing, tutoring, etc.). The longer the list, the better.
2. Determine how many hours per month you can work your side hustle.

3. Begin landing your first few clients and banking that cash!

Kickstarting Your Out Loud Fund

When it comes to your dream, you need to be aggressive about raising the funds needed to make it happen. One strategy to do this is selling unneeded but valuable items via garage sales or online. Designer clothes and accessories in good condition, old textbooks, and even handmade items are a terrific place to start. Even if you make just a few hundred dollars via this strategy, you'll have less clutter and some extra cash to accomplish your goals.

To use this strategy:

1. Collect items that you would like to sell.
2. Decide how you plan to sell these items: Craigslist, eBay, garage sales, etc.
3. List your items and watch the cash roll in.

What About Friends, Family, and Credit Cards?

If bootstrapping and working a side job aren't enough, a last resort is to use credit cards or small business loans, or ask family members for financial support, to launch your dream. Although many use these strategies as a first resort, I list them as a last resort because they complicate your life significantly.

To use this strategy:

1. Determine the exact costs you'll need to finance via credit cards or family loans. Be specific.

2. Create a plan for paying back these loans before you borrow them.
3. Take the needed steps to apply for the loans or ask family and friends for support.

A New Way to See Your 9-5 Job

As mentioned earlier, if you intend to bootstrap your dreams, your job is not your enemy—it's your chief benefactor.

When you take this perspective, every day that you work isn't driving you further from your dream; it's connecting you to your dream. Your job is valuable to your dream in three ways:

1. It provides with you a source of stable funding until your dream is self-sufficient;
2. It provides with you a pool of valuable transferable skills that will also help you on the road to your dream.
3. It provides connections that can be pulled on as you branch out and pursue your dream.

As your dream comes increasingly into focus, you may battle the urge to do the bare minimum from 9-5, so you can save your best thinking, talent, and effort for your dream. Instead of doing the bare minimum, I'd advise you to do the opposite: be the most outstanding worker on the job every single day. Your exceptional work ethic will earn you increased wages and opportunities that will add cash to your dream fund.

What If I Need to Leave My Job?

Sometimes your job *is* a hindrance to living your dream. Examples of this might be a job that requires you to work sixty or more hours per week, is a conflict of interest with your dream, or forbids you to freelance in the area of your dream.

If you *are* set on leaving your job in the near term, there are some steps you absolutely need to take:

- **Prepare your employer for your departure**. I. If you have significant responsibilities in the organization you work for, giving your employer a heads up that this will likely be your last month or your last two weeks with the company is the honorable thing to do. If you cannot share this information without fear of backlash, then at least prepare a transition plan and give as much notice as possible (at least one month, if possible).
- **Save aggressively.** Ensure you have at least one month's living expenses (preferably more) saved in an easy-to-access savings account. Begin curbing expenses to the bare minimum for the transitional point between your last paycheck and your first freelance or dream-related income source.
- **Consider taking a part-time job, rather than becoming completely unemployed.** If at all possible, consider cutting back your work hours or taking a part time job, rather than relying on your dream for 100% of your income. This gives you a steady (albeit smaller) paycheck as you begin to profit from your dream. It also gives you a source of additional cash if needed, by taking additional shifts or projects if your emergency fund dips low.

- **Don't burn bridges.** No matter what, do not burn bridges with a past employer or part-time employer. You'll never know how your previous relationships might be able to help accelerate your dream in the future.

Doing More with Less

This chapter focused on securing funding to jumpstart your dream, but I can't underestimate the need for frugality, creativity, and thrift in the dream-launch process. Even if you have unlimited financial resources backing your dream, the creativity it takes to bring your ideas to light with limited resources sometimes produces equal or better results than what expensive investments in infrastructure or unnecessary "extras" could buy.

Some strategies to accelerate your dream as cheaply as possible include the following:

1. Making sure that every investment you make is absolutely necessary at this point in the dream journey. Although investing in a $300 blog design might *feel* like a great investment, if you haven't even written your first blog post, it might be a bit premature.
2. Bartering professional services with others who need your skills or services in order to cut costs before you turn a profit.
3. Using free versions of products when you are first starting out and upgrading once you begin monetizing your dream.

Looking for discounts, coupons, or used versions of needed capital to save on infrastructure purchases that you will eventually upgrade.

What changes will you make in the next week in order to fund your dream?

~~~~~~~~

Dreamer Spotlight: Langston Hughes and the Truth about Keeping Your Day Job

As a young man, famous African American poet Langston Hughes found the money to make ends meet working a full-time job as a busboy at the Wardman Park Hotel. His job, waiting tables, was not a glamorous one, but it gave him the opportunity to land his big break as a poet.

One day, Hughes had the good fortune to serve the table of poet Vachel Lindsay. While bringing out his meal, Hughes was able to secure a handful of pages of his poetry. He placed the poems by the man's dish and Vachel, although obviously annoyed, read them. Vachel was so impressed, he immediately asked Hughes who wrote them. When Hughes shared that he had authored the poems, Vachel vowed to connect him with the right people to get his career off the ground.

If Langston Hughes hadn't been at the Wardman Hotel that evening, who knows when and if anyone would have ever discovered his writing talents? If his story proves anything, it's that your full-time job might not be the enemy of you accomplishing your dream: it might be a needed stepping stone to get there.

It's easy to believe, when you're working 40 hours a week at a job you don't enjoy, that your job itself is the biggest obstacle to you accomplishing your dreams. If only you had eight hours every day to devote to the thing you love; if only you could get out more, network more, market more. For dreamers whose dreams are at a standstill, this argument is even more convincing: my job doesn't give me the creative thinking space I need to be successful. It's a convenient enemy to blame when our lives aren't working out the way we want them to.

Here are a few thoughts to consider:

1. Even if you are working 45-55 hours a week, you have five-ten hours each week that you can use at your own personal discretion. Are you using that time well? If not, it makes sense that a change in employment would make no difference in how consistently you devote time to your dreams.

2. If you quit your job and had no source of income, other than your dream, how stressful would that be for you? How much time might you obsess over securing resources, paying rent, or finding "odd jobs" that pay less per hour than your salary in order to meet your basic needs? In short, how much of your thought-space and time would you spend on worrying? If you're like most people, the stress of "making ends meet" would leave you with less time to work on your dream than you realize.

3. Has your current job taught you skills transferable to living your dreams out loud? For example, does your career as a receptionist teach you about customer service,

managing up, or setting priorities? Does your job managing a small team teach you how to grow people's skills or give you market insight into how junior employees approach work? For many of us, our full-time jobs are not the enemy of our dream; they're a vital stepping stone to walking our dream out.

In what ways could your current full-time job actually assist you in achieving your dream?

Dreamer Spotlight: Pam Slim and Patience

Until 1996, Pam Slim's life seemed to be going in a steady and predictable corporate direction: she had an amazing job at Barclay's Global Investors, she made an incredible salary, and she'd achieved career success that many women only dreamed of. Despite her career success, Pam wasn't happy. She knew there was something more for her out there.

So, she made a plan to quit her job and pursue something else. After quitting her job, business was slow moving. Pam was stuck. Then, she asked a friend if their company was taking on any consulting/freelance contractors. Once she landed her first job freelancing for that company, the rest was history. Pam became increasingly skilled at landing corporate freelancing work and began coaching others to do the same.

In 2009, Pam published the best-selling book *Escape from Cubicle Nation* to teach others how to transition from corporate employees to self-made entrepreneurs. The book launched

Pam into a fruitful career of speaking, training, and coaching entrepreneurs.

As Pam's story proves, most dreamers' true calling comes into focus over time, unfolding more as they walk the path to pursue it. Rushing the process will not only short-circuit your cash engine but it will also prevent the self-discovery necessary to succeed at your dream.

If Pam had rushed into starting a corporate training business, she might not have realized how much she enjoyed contract work. If she'd written the book too early, she wouldn't have the base of experience and knowledge to prove her expertise. If she quit years before in her career, she wouldn't have had the skill sets needed to take her first round of consulting jobs. By walking out her dream process, step-by-step, Pam created opportunities for herself that were appropriate to where she was on her journey.

Welcome to the Start of Your New Journey

I authored this book because I know from experience that you don't have to settle: you can have the life you want, on your terms. You do not have to wake up anxious and resentful about anything in life, especially a job that you may not enjoy. You do not have to accept a life that lacks excitement and pleasure, or a life that leaves you unfulfilled because you aren't doing work that is meaningful to you. You don't have to be average.

Now, it's your turn: you have to do the work to gain clarity, to obtain the right connections, to be committed, to cultivate competence, to condition your mind, and to secure cash-flow.

1. **Get Clear:** Clear your mind and focus on your most profitable ideas and passions. As mentioned in Module 1, having an understanding of what you genuinely want is the most important thing to give you the blueprint for your success.

2. **Learn to Connect:** Master the art of making friends, finding mentors, and partnering with allies to support your dreams.

3. **Demonstrate Commitment:** Dig deep and commit to doing whatever **is needed** to accomplish your goals.

4. **Cultivate Competence:** Develop your talents and skills to be truly elite at your dream. Put in the work to be better than average and to reap better than average results.

5. **Condition Yourself for Success:** Develop the physical strength, emotional resilience, and mental toughness to pursue even the most challenging dream.

6. **Master Cash Flow:** Have a plan for financing your dream, to ensure your long-term success.

This book is meant to be a starting point on your dream journey. It is just the beginning. Now, it's time for you to follow the instructions you've received, adding your own experience and knowledge along the way, until you reach your desired result.

If you want to dive deeper, or if you want more help along the way, my monthly membership program or one-on-one coaching offerings might be a great place to start.

Now for your final FREE Training Video:
Please visit
www.LiveYourDreamsOutLoud.com/book-Conclusion

About the Author

Brian Johnson is quickly becoming one of the most inspirational thought leaders of his generation. Brian is an Emmy winning TV producer and an Amazon #1 best-selling author, host and inspirational speaker.

Brian has overcome his own personal challenges including homelessness and intense depression, which almost caused him to take his own life. Brian credits' escaping that tragic moment with giving him clarity about his purpose, and as such has dedicated his life to inspiring others to overcome fears to live the life that they deserve. Brian has committed himself to helping others realize their potential.

In 2014 Brian authored "Live Your Dreams Out Loud" to inspire those who are not pursuing their personal dreams and goals. The book quickly became a bestseller on Amazon.

As a host, Brian is starting to film season two of his interview web series called The Dreamer Series. The series was picked up for distribution through multiple platforms including Apple iTunes, Google Watch and Roku.

Brian's podcast, The Live Your Dreams Out Loud podcast, continues to be a popular download via Sound Cloud. Brian inspires his fans daily via his Daily Inspiration videos, which have become a fan favorite on social media.

Additionally; Brian was recently tapped by the LA based BLeave Network to host a podcast focused on NBA players called NBA Dreamers

As an Emmy Winning talent producer; his rolodex reads like a who's who in Hollywood. He has worked alongside Eddie Murphy, Betty White, Kanye West, Sean P. Diddy Combs, Pastor Joel Osteen, Tyler Perry, Michael Strahan, Jessica Alba, Will Smith, John Legend, Ariana Grande, Seth MacFarlane, Trevor Noah, Shakira, Gwyneth Paltrow, Tracee Ellis Ross, Neil Patrick Harris, Camilla Cabello, Lebron James, Linkin Park, Jeremy Renner, Jon Hamm, and Jamie Foxx.

As a personal coach; Johnson's clients have included notable Fortune 500 companies and some of the largest nonprofits in the U.S.

As an in-demand speaker, Brian has shared his message in front of executives and entrepreneurs around the country. Brian's webinars and coaching sessions regularly sell out to students across the globe.

Join the Dreamer Movement

The Live Your Dreams Out Loud movement is a global effort to inspire other dreamers on the "how" to live your dreams. We've designed a high quality DREAMER t-shirt that is the signature tee that founder Brian wears in order to aspire other dreamers to get involved.

Visit **www.LiveYourDreamsOutLoud.com/Dreamer-Tee**

THE DREAMER SERIES

The Dreamer Series is an interview show that takes viewers on a journey to meet individuals creating real change in the world. Its mission is to educate, entertain and inspire passion in each and every viewer.

Host Brian Johnson travels the across the country interviewing the most inspiring entrepreneurs and extraordinary creatives and influencers.

The Dreamer Series seeks out uncommon inventors, innovators and philanthropists across the country- people that are not afraid to go against the status quo. What makes these people tick? What motivates a person who seemingly has the odds stacked against them to rise above and achieve unparalleled success?

The series is produced by Barrett/Johnson Productions and is available on multiple digital platforms, with the primary destination being YouTube.

For more information or to watch The Dreamer Series, please visit **LiveYourDreamsOutLoud.com/shows**

Live Your Dreams Out Loud University

Live Your Dreams Out Loud University is the eLearning platform by Best Selling Author and speaker Brian D Johnson. The Live Your Dreams Out Loud University was designed to provide a hub of resources and education to any dreamer aspiring to be an entrepreneur, thought leader or conscious creator. The University consists of access to Brian D Johnson, dozens of training classes, webinars, and interviews with successful dreamers as well as tips and best practices.

For more information on Live Your Dreams Out Loud University please visit **LiveYourDreamsOutLoud.com/university**

Live Your Dreams Out Loud Podcast

The Live Your Dreams Out Loud podcast is designed to educate, inspire and entertain the millions of dreamers around the world with stories from those who have demonstrated the qualities of success. These interviews are a deep dive into the highs and lows of each interviewee's journey. Guests come from a wide range of backgrounds and give a raw, authentic and unedited view into the struggles and real-world solutions on the path to entrepreneurship. The Live Your Dreams Out Loud podcast is like a free masterclass for inspiring entrepreneurs.

For More Information On Live Your Dreams Out Loud Podcast visit **LiveYourDreamsOutLoud.com/shows**

Please listen at **Liveyourdreamsoutloud.com/podcast**

One on One Coaching with Brian Johnson

 I specialize in coaching clients into the path of entrepreneurship and identifying career goals. Whether you're a recent college graduate looking for what's next, a beginning or seasoned entrepreneur who is looking to get started or currently stuck in pursuit or an individual transitioning in or out of a job, I will help you create an plan to live the life of your dreams. This comprehensive collaborative plan will allow you to move forward with confidence so that you can manifest your dreams. With my unique approach, sense of humor and optimism, I will help you transform your obstacles into opportunities.

For More Information on One On One Coaching with Brian Johnson visit **LiveYourDreamsOutLoud.com/Coaching**